PARTS UNKNOWN

PARTS UNKNOWN

*A Naturalist's Journey in
Search of Birds and Wild Places*

Tim Gallagher

THE LYONS PRESS
Guilford, Connecticut
An imprint of The Globe Pequot Press

The Lyons Press is an imprint of the Globe Pequot Press.

Printed in the United States of America

2 4 6 8 10 9 7 5 3 1

Design by Compset, Inc.

Library of Congress Cataloging-in-Publication Data

Gallagher, Tim.
    Parts unknown : a naturalist's journey in search of birds and wild places
    /Tim Gallagher. p. cm.
    ISBN 1-58574-275-9
    1. Bird watching. 2. Gallagher, Tim—Journeys. I. Title.

QL677.5.G35 2001
598′.07′234092—dc21
[B]

                                                            2001029787

For my mother, Daphne

From Qeqertaq we sailed off into parts unknown.

—Peter Freuchen

CONTENTS

Contents

III
BIRDING AND ORNITHOLOGY

PARTS UNKNOWN

INTRODUCTION

As a child I once went to see a museum exhibit of early maps. Some were nearly half a millennium old—beautiful, ornately drawn charts, tattered from long use, helping guide seamen across vast expanses of open ocean in wood-hulled sailing vessels. What many of these maps had in common was a massive blank area to the north labeled PARTS UNKNOWN, often with a sketch of an Eskimo hunter holding a harpoon. The idea of completely unknown areas was mind-boggling and fired my ten-year-old imagination with visions of exploration and great adventure. I determined then and there that I'd someday figure out a way to get to some of these places, wherever they lay, and see all the amazing birds and other wildlife they held.

I don't think any of this surprised my parents. I come from a family of wanderers. In the late nineteenth century my grandfather on my dad's side joined the Royal Marines as an eight-year-old drummer boy. These boys traditionally stood on the decks of warships in the thick of battle, beating drums to inspire the men as cannonballs whizzed past. He was aboard a British naval vessel in Havana Harbor during the Spanish-American War—there, along with the ships of other neutral nations, to protect national interests. He was so young when he joined up that when he retired after being a "lifer" in the marines, he was only in his twenties. The first thing he did was sign up on the crew of a big sailing ship owned by an English lord and head off to Hawaii (then called the Sandwich Islands).

Just a baby when his father left, my dad was a restless three-year-old by the time he returned. He squirmed in his mother's arms as she held him up to look at everyone coming down the ship's gangplank. He pointed at each man and said: "Is that my dad? Is that my dad?"

But it wasn't long before my dad also started itching to leave. At age eleven he tried to run away and join the Royal Navy, and he succeeded by the time he was fifteen. This caused something of a scandal in my family. You see, all of the Gallagher men since the days of Horatio Nelson had been Royal Marines—until my dad decided to become a common sailor. To appreciate what this meant, you have to remember that the marines had originally been formed largely to keep the sailors in line. They paraded on deck with nice red uniforms and muskets, ready to hammer any seaman who became rebellious or disorderly in any way—and the sailors of Nelson's time were a motley crew of sea dogs, grabbed from the grimiest wharves and backwaters of the empire. Without the marines, the officers could never have maintained order. Although things had changed a lot by the time my dad joined up, the marines still tended to look down on sailors. And here was my dad, in his midteens, joining up with that rabble. I don't know much about the other Gallagher men before my grandfather, but I do have some interesting pictures of my great-grandfather. One is a formal portrait of him in the full-dress uniform of a Royal Marine. (He looked a lot like my dad.) And the other, my favorite, shows him with two other young marines, all of them perched atop camels in front of the pyramids in Egypt.

For my dad it must have been exciting running around in Shanghai and other exotic places at the age of sixteen, free of his parents, beholden only to King George and the lords of the Admiralty. But it wasn't all good. It was in the navy that he picked up his lifelong addictions to tobacco and drink—which eventually cost him his family, his health, and, ultimately, his life.

The timing of his enlistment was particularly bad—in the late 1930s, shortly before England declared war on Germany. The Royal Navy was on the front lines immediately in 1939, months before the Royal Air Force got into the fray in the Battle of Britain. Really the only reason the Germans needed to launch an air war against England was that the Royal Navy presented such a formidable obstacle to invasion. So the ships my dad served on were rushed here and there, wherever a convoy needed protection, wherever a port needed to be blockaded. He made long journeys through frigid seas to supply Soviet ports—sitting for hours at the guns, shivering from the cold and frequently strafed by Luftwaffe planes. Once a German plane came in low across the sea, headed straight for him, firing its guns. Bullets ricocheted all around him, creating flaming sparks as they slammed into the armor plating. Miraculously, he was untouched—but dead sailors lay all around him, including his best friend, who sat beside him at the same gun, a bullet hole in his forehead and a serene smile on his face: an image my father would carry for the rest of his life. He was sunk three times and each time received a two-week "survivor's leave." He met my mother on one of those leaves.

For the British and most other Europeans during World War II, the people back home were often in as much danger as those actually fighting. It was certainly so for my family. My grandfather on my mother's side, Frank Hide Munks, was killed by a German bomb in 1940 on the streets of my hometown while he was on patrol—he was a wartime reserve policeman in Sheffield, England. He was about the same age as I am now. One night the office building where my mother worked was leveled in an air raid—fortunately when no one was inside. Her eldest brother, also named Frank, died shortly after his father. A recently enlisted British sailor, he was aboard a ship sunk by a U-boat while it was escorting a convoy across the North Atlantic.

But my dad's wanderlust didn't leave him after the war, which is why his three children were born in such far-apart places—my older sister, Maureen, in Malta; me in England; and my younger sister, Janet, in Canada. I'll never forget the trip from England to Quebec—a late-night train ride to

Southampton on a steam locomotive, followed by an ocean voyage on an aging Greek liner. I remember seeing a few tiny houses along the shore as we traveled up the St. Lawrence River toward Montreal, and for some reason I thought it was the coast of Africa—perhaps because my aunt and uncle had been visiting us from Northern Rhodesia just before we left England. For at least a couple of years after that journey I thought that we'd come by way of Africa—definitely the long way around to get to Canada.

My dad had come to Canada quite a while earlier to get established with a job and a place to live before he sent for us. But he was still restless. We moved several times during the six years we were in Canada, and then he got it into his head that we should move to another country again—to either the United States or Mexico. We applied for immigrant status in both countries. Now that I think back, it might have been interesting if we had ended up south of the border. If nothing else, I'm sure I'd have become a much better Spanish speaker.

Anyway, for better or worse, we moved to the United States in time to see a missile crisis almost launch us into World War III, a president shot down in the streets of an American city, and an ugly war start that left many of my friends maimed, physically and emotionally—but that's another story.

It took a few more years before I started my own independent travels. From the start my journeys were always bird related. I had been interested in wild birds since before I even started grade school. I watched them and occasionally raised young birds that fell from nests. But it wasn't until I took up falconry at the age of twelve that my interest in birds really blossomed. Although I was officially too young to train a falcon, the wildlife laws were much more lax in the early 1960s, and I was able to get a falconry permit in my mother's name. At that time raptors had not yet been bred in captivity, even though falconers had trained and handled these birds for centuries. To get a hawk, you had to learn everything you could about the natural history and habits of a species so that you could find a nest or trap one. On weekends in spring I would ride my bike into the hills, then hide it and hike for miles, returning perhaps fifteen hours later, weary and weather beaten. I found lots of nesting raptors on those day trips: Golden Eagles, White-tailed Kites, Great Horned Owls, Burrowing Owls—birds I had no interest in training but were fascinating to study just the same. Sadly, the areas where I found all of these nests have since been developed. To look at them now, with their wall-to-wall condominiums and malls, you'd never know how special they once were.

I also found nesting American Kestrels and Red-tailed Hawks. These I did fly, and I did well with them. At the end of the season I'd release them back into the wild, thereby getting them most of the way through their difficult first year, when nine out of ten young raptors perish.

When I was sixteen a friend of mine and I decided we wanted to drive all the way from Southern California to South Dakota in a beat-up old car to attend the annual meeting of the North American Falconers' Association. Rich was a year older than me and kind of a hood. He lived in Long Beach and drove a lowered '49 Chevy. His mother had seen me walking home from a field one afternoon, carrying my trained Red-tailed Hawk on my fist. She stopped her car and told me that her son had always been interested in falconry. Rich and I got together soon after. Up to that point I'd had to walk, ride a bicycle, or hitchhike with my bird to get to fields where I could let her hunt rabbits. Rich started driving me to new hunting areas. It was great. Sometimes, though, he'd come over driving his dad's tiny red Austin Healy. It was quite a challenge motoring along the freeway with a huge, restless Red-tailed Hawk in the front seat of a sports car.

My parents had recently gotten divorced, and I think my mother was trying to let me have more freedom; I certainly didn't have much when my dad lived with us. Amazingly, she said I could go to South Dakota—even though I'd be gone for a couple of weeks, including Thanksgiving Day, and miss some school—and for that I am eternally grateful.

So a week later we were on our way, putt-putting and grinding our way south—yes, south; we were trying to bypass as much as possible of the cold weather and high mountains we would have faced on the northern route. We chose to travel the soft underbelly of America—Route 66—heading through Arizona, New Mexico, and part of Texas before turning due north through Oklahoma, Kansas, Nebraska, and on into eastern South Dakota to a small city called Centerville.

It was not all smooth sailing. Our engine had a small oil leak that drip, drip, dripped tiny specks of greasy black liquid onto the highway across eight states. Whenever we stopped at a service station, we'd say, "Fill her up with oil and check the gas." We wore out a front-wheel bearing at one point, and Rich got bitten by a big dog as he swiped a replacement bearing from an old truck in a pile of rusting cars in the desert. The muffler was falling apart, making the car sound like a top-fuel dragster as we rumbled through each tiny berg.

One small-town deputy sheriff in New Mexico came running out of a café with a napkin still tucked in his shirt and stood in front of our car to stop us. "Why aren't you in school?" he snarled, ketchup dripping down his chin.

"It's Saturday," I replied.

"Yeah, but you didn't leave home this morning!"

True . . . but somehow we finessed our way out of it—or, I should say, Rich did. He was smooth. The man finally wished us luck on our trip, turned, and strode back into the café. Rich slowly pulled out a comb and dragged his Brylcreamed dishwater-blond hair back, carefully making it stand up in front, Long Beach hood style. Slipping on his shades, he lit up a Camel, smirked at me, then fired up the engine—*vrroooom, vrrooom*—and we were off, with nothing left to stop us.

We continued on . . . for days, it seemed. Sleeping in the car. Living on cans of beans that we put on top of the engine as we drove to warm them up. I guess I hadn't told my mom that we didn't have enough money for food—just gas and oil. And Rich taught me the trick of sitting at the counter at a truck-stop café and ordering a cup of tea. Instead of dropping the teabag into the little hot-water container, though, he would pour half a bottle of ketchup into it, salt and pepper it liberally, and voilà!—instant tomato soup, with plenty of crackers at the table for filler. After finishing the meal, he would wipe the container out with his napkin, then ask for a refill of water, which he would use to make a real cup of tea. Only problem was, the tea tasted like Heinz ketchup.

The falconry meet was great. And the town of Centerville seemed genuinely pleased to host the group. In the window of the local bakery stood a massive cake with a stooping falcon and WELCOME FALCONERS! emblazoned across it in decorative icing. All the greats of the sport were there, including the famous British falconer and author Jack Mavrogordato—who was just like some old-time Victorian gentleman and had lived for years in the Sudan, flying Lanners, Sakers, and other exotic falcons.

But what made the meet most interesting to me was that it took place just the year after the famed Peregrine Falcon conference in 1965, convened by ornithologist Joe Hickey at the University of Wisconsin. Falcon researchers from around the world had converged on Madison to compare notes and examine the Peregrine Falcon's plight. They learned that the situation was much worse than anyone had expected; that the bird had already been extirpated as a breeding species in the entire eastern United States. A number of key figures who had been at that conference (Fran Hammerstrom, Jim Enderson, Heinz Meng, Frank Beebe, Dan Berger and others) were in attendance at the falconry meet, continuing the discussion they'd begun a year earlier, and it was fascinating to hear them speak. It was also shocking; I'd had no idea we were in such imminent danger of losing the Peregrine Falcon.

Rich and I would come out of those discussions wide eyed and then realize that we had to find a place to sleep. We didn't have enough money for a hotel room, though I think they were only four or five bucks a night in town. We spent one night in an abandoned building in an old park, but I couldn't sleep—I could hear a raccoon or other animal walking around all night, and it kept stopping right in front of my face. The next night we slept beside a river with Jim Weaver and another falconer from Illinois. A few years later Jim would head The Peregrine Fund's falcon-breeding facility at Cornell University; a lot of the success of the Peregrine Falcon reintroduction in North America is thanks to his efforts. Jim had fairly recently returned from Alaska, and he had two nice peregrines—an adult female and a first-year male—perched next to his sleeping bag. His friend had a beautiful gray Gyrfalcon, the first I had ever seen.

Jim looked like a real mountain man, with a huge bushy mustache and wild, dark red hair. He was definitely in his element in that cold. Rich and I . . . well, we'd come from a balmy climate and had thin sleeping bags. I'd had mine since I was a Cub Scout and it only came up to my chest. And it was cold out . . . damn cold . . . South Dakota cornfield cold. I was shivering so much that the rattling of my bones kept me awake—so I lost another night's sleep. By the time we got up in the morning, the river beside us had frozen solidly enough to skate on.

Rich and I shambled around town the next morning like shell-shocked refugees, dark rings beneath our eyes. We paused outside the bakery, gazing longingly at the falconry cake inside. The next thing we knew, the woman who worked there had waved us inside and given us some free Danish rolls. She got excited when she found out we were from California; her daughter lived there. She asked where we were staying, and we mumbled something about the trees outside of town. Then she invited us to stay at her place with her husband, a retired farmer. We were in heaven. He was a hunter and she, a fabulous cook. We ate pheasant, venison, and homemade apple pie every night. And it was warm.

Later, as we left to drive back to California, she handed us two grocery bags full of day-old Danish rolls—and that's all we ate for five days. I've never liked Danish rolls since.

That trip to South Dakota was a long time ago, but I've described it in such detail here because it was one of those watershed moments in life—I knew this even as I was living it. The adventure of it all. Jumping into the unknown; heading down the road, ready or not. Fixing things when we had to; finding food anywhere we could. All that, and I was also exploring and learning about things that would be important to me for the rest of my life—the falcons, the bird research. And I knew that I would see the people I met on that trip again and again. That single journey, back in 1966, launched me firmly on a road that I am still traveling to this day.

Not long after returning from South Dakota, I started taking shorter trips with some of my high school friends—Mac, Robert, and Hollis—to Arizona, Nevada, and all through the California deserts, searching for nesting Prairie Falcons and other wildlife. There I learned to climb and rappel down sheer cliff faces: the only way to reach most falcon nests. And I started dreaming of even more faraway places.

Of course, all the blank spots on the maps had been filled in long before I was born, but I still wanted to see interesting places with my own eyes— places that were still "parts unknown" to me. I started traveling under my own steam, hitchhiking cross-country or scraping together enough gas money to drive to far-off destinations with friends. Right out of high school, a friend of mine and I drove an old pickup truck to the grasslands of western Canada and then farther north all the way to Yellowknife, Northwest Territories—as far as that old gravel highway would take us. Once again, we had enough money for only gas and oil—not food, lodging, or camp fees. We slept wherever we could find a nice pull-off or a clump of trees to hide the truck, and we lived on road-kill grouse and trout that we stopped to catch in rivers and creeks. And while we were driving through central Alberta, we followed behind potato trucks; whenever they crossed a railroad track, a dozen or so fat spuds would roll off the top of the pile and fall onto the road, where we'd snatch them up.

Eventually I started hooking up with bird researchers, working with them in the field, taking pictures and writing articles about the birds they studied and my experiences. Over the years I've gone to some great places. I've scaled huge cliffs in Northern Greenland and Iceland to look at young Gyrfalcons while their parents screamed and dived at my head. I've climbed lofty trees to reach Golden Eagle nests and sat in the massive stick structures with nearly grown young. I've trapped migrating Arctic Peregrine Falcons on barrier islands in the Gulf of Mexico as the birds made their way to their wintering grounds in South America. And I've written numerous essays about these places and their wildlife. A selection of them appears here.

But these essays are not all about wild, exotic places. Some of them tell the story of the birds I've followed—the falcons, condors, and others—because trying to help these birds and make their plight known to the world at large has been the catalyst that's driven so much of my nature writing and traveling. And some of these essays deal with places that at first glance seem mundane—areas that stand side by side with or even inside large cities, because these places are important, too. And they contain unknown elements for anyone who has enough sensitivity and knowledge to appreciate them. I'm reminded of one of my favorite passages from Aldo Leopold's *A Sand County Almanac:*

> Every July I watch eagerly a certain country graveyard that I pass in driving to and from my farm. . . . It is an ordinary graveyard, bordered by the usual spruces, and studded with the usual pink granite or white marble headstones, each with the usual Sunday bouquet of red or pink geraniums. It is extraordinary only in being triangular instead of square, and in harboring, within the sharp angle of its fence, a pin-point remnant of the native prairie on which the graveyard was established in the 1840s. Heretofore unreachable by scythe or mower, this yard-square relic of original Wisconsin gives birth, each July, to a man-high stalk of compass plant or cutleaf Silphium, spangled with saucer-sized yellow blooms resembling sunflowers. It is the sole remnant of this plant along this highway, and perhaps the sole remnant in the western half of our county. What a thousand acres of Silphium looked like when they tickled the bellies of the buffalo is a question never again to be answered, or perhaps not even asked.

In that tiny yard-square triangle of "weeds," Leopold found a fragment of the wild earth worth knowing—a relic of the prairie that once blanketed the en-

tire area for hundreds and hundreds of miles. Things like this are "parts unknown," wherever you can find them.

For many years I watched vital habitats disappearing all around me in
Southern California. I remember sitting in fields and tiny wetlands along
Pacific Coast Highway—often right in among the surveyor's stakes that designated the areas slated for development—where I'd photograph these forgotten, soon-to-be-obliterated worlds: Black-necked Stilts sitting on their eggs;
Cinnamon Teal foraging in the shallows; American Avocets striding past,
sweeping their long curved bills from side to side. I wanted to preserve whatever fragments I could, even if they were only photographic images, to document what we had lost.

I'm glad we didn't lose all the battles. I'm glad the housing developments
that threatened to spill over and overwhelm Back Bay Newport in the 1960s
were halted in their tracks at the top of the cliffs. It's great to be able to report
that positive things are taking place in sensitive areas like Back Bay Newport,
Catalina Island, Elk Island, and the Everglades.

As I write this introduction, I'm getting ready to leave on a research trip to
the ice off northern Alaska, where I'll help monitor whales and other remarkable Arctic wildlife. I seem to have a need to keep returning to remote areas
like these. The exposure to wilderness renews me in some profound way. But I
hope I'll also always be capable of seeing the "parts unknown" in my own
backyard.

—Tim Gallagher
Freeville, New York
March 2001

I

PARTS UNKNOWN

1

ICELAND
JOURNAL

June 1998

Waiting at the tiny bus station in Reykjavik, Iceland, I feel like someone who has arranged to meet a blind date but forgotten to ask what the person looks like. I know nothing about Olafur Nielsen's appearance. We've been sending e-mails back and forth for several months to set up my trip to Iceland, where I'll accompany him as he conducts field research on Gyrfalcons. But neither of us thought to ask for a description of the other, or to arrange for a visual clue: "Look for the guy with the Gyrfalcon feather stuck in his hat." I know only that Olafur is a native Icelander, about my age, who received a Ph.D. in ornithology from Cornell University in the mid-1980s (working as a graduate student with former Lab of Ornithology research director and Peregrine Fund founder Tom Cade), and that he is now an animal ecologist at the Icelandic Institute of Natural History in Reykjavik.

In the waiting room sit a dozen or more Icelanders—some in silence, staring out the window or quietly puffing on cigarettes, others engaged in lively conversations. I try listening to them, hoping to get an idea of what they're saying. I've studied French, Latin, Anglo-Saxon, and some German; I figure I should be able to pick out an occasional familiar word. Nothing. They may as well be saying, "Blah, blah, blah, blah." I do notice, though, that their sentences are punctuated occasionally with a word that sounds like "yow," which seems to be some kind of affirmative, like "yeah."

Then I see two men, both in their early forties, enter the room—a tall, thin man with glasses and graying hair and another, shorter man, with longish ginger-brown hair and the scruffy start of a beard. They split up and walk around the room, looking closely at each person—but, curiously, they go right past me as if I'm invisible. Instead of taking a direct approach and asking who they are, I pull out a field guide and open it to a color plate of a Gyrfalcon. Noticing the book, the shorter of the two grabs the other man by the sleeve and points at me. "Are you Olafur Nielsen?" I ask, resisting the impulse to say, "Dr. Nielsen, I presume." The taller man says yes and we shake hands. He introduces the other man as his field assistant, Dany Pierret, a Belgian who's been living in Iceland for the past two years.

It's amazing how quickly we get down to the business of the trip. After coffee at Olafur's house with his wife, we whisk away to the nearby domestic airport and catch a one-hour flight to Akureyri, in northeastern Iceland, pick up a four-wheel-drive truck owned by the institute, load up on supplies, and are on our way into the hinterlands. Less than two hours later we're driving up a steep, rocky hill en route to a Gyrfalcon eyrie. Before we get there, though, we stop at a sheep farmer's house; the tiny dirt road leading to the eyrie runs right past his yard and through his sheep pens. As he comes out his front door, he seems genuinely pleased to see Olafur. "Blah, blah, blah, blah?" he says. "Yow, blah, blah, blah, yow," Olafur replies.

Though the man has the thick, dark brown hair of a young man, his face looks ancient—a little like Ronald Reagan. Later, as we drop in on more and more of these sheep farmers in the course of our trip, I see that many of them have this same general look: great hair, wrinkled faces. Whether they are young men whose faces have been battered and shriveled by harsh weather or old men whose hair has been miraculously preserved, I have no idea. Olafur talks to the man for perhaps thirty minutes. This, I also soon find out, will be the routine most places we go. Even in remote areas, a sheep farmer's land is often the gateway to Gyrfalcon country. If we're lucky, a brief chat with the landowner is all we need to get past his farmhouse; if we aren't so lucky, we might have to spend a couple of hours drinking coffee and listening to the rhythmic patter of these—for Dany and me—incomprehensible Icelandic conversations.

Dany has been taking a class in Icelandic for two years now. But even though he's already fluent in two or three languages, the Icelandic tongue remains a mystery to him. "None of it makes sense," he tells me. "Even Norwegians don't understand it when they come here, and their language evolved from this one." The Norse language of the Icelanders, I find out, has remained virtually unchanged since the original Viking settlers brought it here more than a millennium ago.

We finally leave the farmer and drive for several miles. When we reach a point where the boulders and sharp volcanic rocks make it impossible to drive any farther, we park the truck and make our way on foot up a steep hill to get above the nest—on a rock ledge high on the side of a narrow gorge with a glacial river running through it. Carrying a pack full of heavy camera gear and a tripod, I stagger up the slope, twenty feet behind Olafur and Dany, who are practically running. (I guess sitting at a computer and taking a stroll through Sapsucker Woods Sanctuary once a day is a poor preparation for this kind of physical activity.)

Gyrfalcons almost always nest on cliffs, usually the higher the better, giving them a commanding view of the surrounding area. They tend to lay their eggs on grassy ledges or in stick nests built by ravens in previous years. The falcons never build a nest, though they may make a small scrape in the soft earth of a ledge to hold their eggs. Getting to a Gyrfalcon nest, or eyrie, usually involves making a precarious climb to the top of a cliff and then rappelling down a rope to reach the nest ledge.

As we reach the top of the cliff, an adult female Gyrfalcon makes several power dives at us, screaming harshly as she flies past. Despite the roar of rushing water, her voice echoes through the canyon, sounding like a rusty pump broadcast over a public address system. The male—a pale, silver-gray beauty—sits on a grassy slope across the river, screaming from afar.

Dany unfurls the climbing rope, ties the end around his waist, and throws the rest of it over the cliff. He then sits down, becoming a human anchor for the rope. Olafur tells me he will band the young falcons inside the nest, instead of bringing them up and having to climb the cliff again. There's no place to stand at the bottom of the cliff—it ends right in the river—so Olafur will swing out over the water and come down on the other side. I'm not sure exactly how he intends to get back, but I nod and get ready to snap some pictures of him, though the freezing wind and dark skies are lousy conditions for photography. Olafur hands me a walkie-talkie encased in a waterproof pouch with a rope to hang it around my neck and then disappears over the cliff.

Looking down, I think back on the times as a teenager when my best friend Mac would tell me make-believe newspaper headlines—just as I was backing off a cliff to rappel to a Golden Eagle eyrie: BOY, 16, FALLS TO DEATH AT EAGLE NEST.

After fifteen or twenty minutes Olafur radios that he's at the bottom on the other side, and we should pull up the rope. It's difficult to hear over the river noise. It sounds like he's saying that I should make my way down the steep talus slope through a break in the cliff to get to the edge of the water and then dangle the end of the rope downstream until it reaches him. I ask him to repeat the message a couple of times to make sure I'm hearing him correctly. "It sounds like he wants me to drag him across the river with a rope," I tell Dany. "Does that seem right to you?" Dany looks blank and shrugs.

Hoisting the rope over my shoulder, I start toward the river. The rocks underfoot are small, sharp, and loose—completely broken. I try to hold the sides as I go down, but I slip a couple of times, sending an avalanche of small rocks tumbling and plunging into the icy river. The loose rock slope below me disappears right into the water. I'm wondering where I will stand when I reach the bottom. Olafur's voice keeps blasting over the walkie-talkie. *"Blah, blah, blah, blah!"* He might as well be speaking Icelandic; I can't hear a thing over the river noise. At the water's edge I lean hard against the edge of the cliff and throw the rope with all my might toward the other side of the river. The current takes it and carries it downstream. Dany comes up behind me a few minutes later, and we both hold the end of the rope.

Suddenly, *slam!* It feels like we've hooked a 170-pound salmon. We can barely hold the rope against the force of the current. Then we spot Olafur, making his way across the frigid, rushing river, dressed only in briefs—his clothes, boots, and equipment are stashed in a rucksack on his back. With water breaking over his shoulders at times, he walks hand-over-hand along the rope.

Almost all the people you meet in Iceland—especially the farmers—are aware of the Gyrfalcon, or *falki,* as it is called there. It's the national bird, but it seems even more important than that. I think Icelanders identify with this fierce, silver-gray warrior. Perhaps it's part of their Viking heritage. Icelanders tend to be extremely protective of these birds. If a farmer sees someone approaching a Gyrfalcon eyrie, he'll invariably call the police. That's one reason Olafur always checks in with farmers as he's making the rounds of Gyrfalcon eyries.

Even the children in Iceland know about Gyrfalcons. A friend of mine was traveling through the country a couple of years ago when he spotted a Gyrfalcon diving at phalaropes along the shore of a small lake, not far from the spot where a twelve-year-old girl and her younger brother were standing. My friend, who happened to be wearing a Peregrine Fund T-shirt with a flying Peregrine Falcon pictured on the front, called excitedly to the children.

"Falcon . . . falcon . . . see? Like this," he said, pointing at his shirt.

The girl shook her head. "No, no."

"Yes, falcon," he insisted.

"No, *peregrinus*," she said, pointing at his shirt. Then, turning and pointing toward the Gyrfalcon, which was still buzzing the phalaropes nearby, she said "*rusticolus*," correctly identifying the scientific names of both birds.

The Icelanders' relationship with the Gyrfalcon goes back to the Middle Ages, when these prized birds were exported to emperors and kings across Europe, where they were used for falconry. This practice continued right up to the French Revolution. The Danish king (Denmark ruled Iceland at that time) actually had a shipment of Icelandic Gyrfalcons ready to send to Louis XVI at the time he was snatched and eventually guillotined by the rebels.

It's not surprising that Gyrfalcons have always been prized by falconers. They're spectacular hunters, with speed and stamina unsurpassed by any other raptor. Although Peregrine Falcons are famous for diving like meteors from colossal heights to clobber their prey, they lack the Gyrfalcon's ability to take off like a rocket and pursue prey unrelentingly in level or rising flight. And the Gyrfalcon's endurance is legendary. I once saw one take off from a dead standstill, near ground level, and tail-chase a drake Canvasback until it caught it, more than a mile away—an impossible feat for a peregrine. Gyrfalcons often cruise fast and low over the vast Arctic spaces, just waiting for an unlucky ptarmigan to appear. And Gyrfalcons are huge: twenty-five inches in length, compared with twenty inches for the Peregrine Falcon.

In medieval Europe the quarry of choice for trained Gyrfalcons was the Grey Heron—a bird similar in general appearance to a Great Blue Heron. Falconers would release their birds as the herons were flying past high overhead, en route to or from their feeding areas, and the falcons would fly after them, circling up powerfully as they fought to gain an altitude advantage over the larger birds. These flights would sometimes continue for miles, with the royal spectators following at full gallop on horseback. After their capture, the herons were often rescued by the falconers and released after a copper band (with the name of the falcon's owner and the year engraved on it) had been affixed to the bird's leg. Some were caught again and again over the years. This may well have been the earliest examples of both bird banding and a "catch-and-release" field sport.

From the front window of Olafur's home in Reykjavik, you can see the home of his country's president, across the water on a small spit of land. At one time this is where the falcons were taken prior to being shipped to Copenhagen and then distributed to the royal courts of Europe. Curiously, the Icelanders never developed a tradition of falconry in their own country.

Olafur has had an avid interest in birds since childhood. As a teenager, growing up in Reykjavik, he became friends with Finnur Gudmundsson, the father of Icelandic ornithology. Working as a field assistant with Gudmundsson in the early 1970s sparked Olafur's interest in Gyrfalcon and ptarmigan research. When he entered graduate school at Cornell University in 1980, Olafur—in association with Cornell professor Tom Cade—began a Gyrfalcon study in northeastern Iceland that continues to the present.

When he started this research, Olafur drove all over the countryside in his study area, talking with farmers and asking them if they knew where falcons nested. Many did, especially if the eyries were on or near their property. He documented more than eighty traditional Gyrfalcon territories, and he checks them at least once each spring. If the nests are active, he'll come back in late June to band and measure the young, and again in August to see how many young falcons have fledged.

The land is rugged, with miles of jagged volcanic rock, making it difficult to visit and climb to more than two or three nests a day. It is meticulous, painstaking work. Some of the cliffs are too treacherous to climb: lofty cascades of sharp, rope-cutting lava rock, with overhangs above the nest ledges. At these nests he uses a spotting scope to count the young.

It's funny; my first impression on meeting Olafur was that he is stolid and reserved—the quintessential Icelander. But I was completely wrong, about Olafur *and* his countrymen. On the back roads of Iceland, he is as gregarious as a traveling salesman, striding easily up to any farmstead, no matter how remote and at practically any time of day and night (no one there sleeps at night in the summer anyway), and engaging the farmers in lengthy conversations. Many farmers in these remote areas are starved for contact with other people and for news from other parts of the country. Iceland has an incredibly small human population—not much more than a quarter of a million total—and the vast majority of them live in or near Reykjavik. These sheep farmers are about as cut off from civilization as you can get and still live in a house. Olafur has been making the rounds of Gyrfalcon eyries in this area practically since he was a teenager, and he's well known by the locals.

We stand on the banks of the largest glacial river I've yet seen here—a massive body of water flowing hundreds of miles from a glacier far to the south. A great island with a sheer cascade of cliffs rises like an immense wall in the center of the river. Olafur explains that the only way for us to reach the eyrie is to wade across the river and around to the other side of the island, following it upstream a mile or so until we reach an area with a gradual slope that will allow us to climb on top of the island and make our way to the nest cliff. Olafur tells me that in the 1930s Hermann Göring sent a crack team of German agents to this very eyrie to get young Gyrfalcons for a national falconry organization he headed. Of course, they used a boat; we don't even have waders. Olafur says it will take four to five hours at least to go there and back—through bone-chilling melted glacial water. It's already past eight o'clock at night and a frigid wind is blowing constantly from the north. Perhaps noticing the look on my face, Olafur mercifully excuses me from this mission. The weather is too bleak for photography anyway.

The last thing I see before I fall asleep in the cab of the truck is Olafur and Dany rounding the end of the island, wading through chest-deep water, trying their best to hold their packs high enough to keep the contents dry. When I wake up five hours later, they are just making their way back to shore. Dany tells me I was wise to stay at the truck. It was awful. His feet are raw and bruised from the stream rocks he's had to stumble across, wearing only socks, and he's chilled to the bone. The cliff the falcons nest on also has a Northern

Fulmar colony, and Olafur just missed being oiled a couple of times by the birds. These pretty white seabirds, with their soft, doelike eyes, can really make a mess of you if they hit you with the noxious, foul-smelling oil they spit on their enemies. More than a few Gyrfalcons have been brought to the institute in Reykjavik helpless and unable to fly after a direct hit with fulmar oil.

Dany is a lot different from Olafur, though they are both interesting field companions. He is an unreformed idealist, with strong views on almost any topic that comes up. He tends to see the world in strict terms of black and white, good and bad, and he reminds me of some of my friends (and myself) in the 1960s. He's also a seeker, constantly searching for the perfect country— one in which the people are in perfect harmony with nature. Dany's travels have so far taken him to the Yukon, where he worked for a year in construction, several countries on the European continent, and now to Iceland, where he's employed as a carpenter and furniture maker. But he's becoming increasingly disillusioned with the attitude he says Icelanders have toward nature: that wildlife is a commodity to be harvested by humans. He is now talking about taking a train ride across Siberia, to see the Arctic from another continent, and then perhaps settling in Finland for a time. He recently heard a story that disturbed him, though, about a bear killed by a Finnish posse— after it had killed a jogger.

"You can't have wild animals killing people in urban areas. No nation in the world would put up with that," Olafur told him one day as we drove across an endless lava field left here by a centuries-old volcanic eruption. "Why not?" said Dany. "There are plenty of people in the world but not, I think, enough bears." Another day he asked me: "The people in New York, are they ecologists?" And I wondered if he was considering another migration, to North America.

Dany is a great field assistant—eager and with boundless energy. An avid birder who loves Gyrfalcons, he first came here with Olafur last year as a volunteer, paying his own way. (Olafur's twenty-one-year-old son was his main field assistant at that time, but he was unable to go out with him this June due to a leg injury.) Olafur called Dany at the last minute before this trip, asking him if he would come along, all expenses paid. Dany agreed and used up most of his allotted vacation time to do so.

Dany visited one Gyrfalcon eyrie last season that had failed for a couple of years in a row. The nest ledge had a northern exposure that offered no protection from the elements when the wind blew from across the Arctic Ocean, bringing frigid temperatures and foul weather. For the past two years snowstorms had come in late June when the young were about three weeks old and too large for the mother falcon to shelter adequately with her body. Both times, all of the young perished. This pair had formerly nested nearby in an old raven's nest on a sheltered cliff face. But the stick nest had fallen apart over the years and become too unstable to accommodate a Gyrfalcon adequately. Dany was so disturbed about what happened to the young falcons that he decided to do something about it. Last winter he took a bus to the site, coming all the way from Reykjavik, then persuaded a local farmer to drive him partway to the nest. When the truck could go no farther, Dany took off overland on foot, across the snow, carrying various sticks, tools, and pieces of wire to the old raven nest. Painstakingly, in bitterly cold weather, he reconstructed the nest, making it sturdy enough to hold anything. He had his reward as we climbed the cliff and saw three large, healthy, four-week-old Gyrfalcons sitting snugly in the stick nest.

At every accessible nest we visit, Olafur weighs each young falcon, measures its beak, wing, and tail-feather length, and writes all the figures down carefully in his notebook. He then scrapes up all of the prey remains from the nest and puts them in a canvas bag. When we get back to the truck, he dumps the bones and feathers on the ground and spreads them out. "Here's a Rock Ptarmigan; this one's an Atlantic Puffin," he says, carefully sorting them and figuring out how many of each species is represented. "Look. Here's a ptarmigan leg with a band on it." He examines the number. "It's one of the ones I banded last winter." He smiles, like he's just met an old friend again.

I ask him about the puffin remains. This eyrie is in a completely dry, desertlike area more than twenty miles from the sea. He tells me that Gyrfalcons routinely hunt long distances from their nests and carry their prey all the way back to their young. In areas like this, they have to. The enormous size of a Gyrfalcon makes it capable of carrying even duck-sized birds great distances. A puffin is easy.

Rock Ptarmigans are an abundant, relatively simple-to-catch food for Gyrfalcons in early spring, when the male ptarmigans are displaying conspicuously everywhere, but the situation changes abruptly come early June. After their courtship displays are over, the male ptarmigans become secretive, spending most of their time hunkered down in cover. They even begin rolling around in small muddy depressions, rubbing red earth onto their sleek white wing feathers. All of a sudden the ptarmigans you see look dirty and unkempt—but they also blend in perfectly with their surroundings. Around June 5 or so the number of fresh ptarmigan carcasses in Gyrfalcon eyries dwindles almost to nil and the seabirds and waterfowl start piling up: Black-legged Kittiwakes, Northern Fulmars, Atlantic Puffins, young Pink-footed Geese, and a variety of ducks. For many pairs, catching these birds means traveling a long way from their home territories.

Though Gyrfalcons have nesting territories that they defend vigorously from intruders, such as other Gyrfalcons, many of the hunting areas appear to be used communally by the birds—especially after the ptarmigans begin hiding. The Lake Myvatn area, for example, probably provides a hunting area for a dozen or more pairs, some of which may nest twenty miles or more away. All of their prey must be carried back this distance to their young.

As Olafur examines prey remains at another eyrie and writes them up in his notebook, I notice a huge pile of old bird bones not far from where he's sitting. For a moment I wonder whether this is a favorite plucking perch for the falcons, but Olafur soon sets me straight. This is where he dumps the remains after inspecting them. I'm seeing the accumulation of nearly twenty years of prey remains from this eyrie alone, and it's impressive—in terms of showing both the hunting prowess of the Gyrfalcons and the depth of Olafur's determination to document these birds' activities on a decades-long scale. This is what is most meaningful and important about his work. He's providing a longitudinal study, over a substantial period of time, of a healthy population of predators and their prey.

Olafur has been able to document the dynamics of the up-and-down population cycles of the falcons and their primary prey species, the Rock Ptarmigan—the Gyrfalcon numbers always shadowing the rising and falling ptarmigan numbers, usually with a year or two delay in between. A picture is beginning to emerge of the close relationship between these two species. Interestingly, the white-phase Gyrfalcons, which come to Iceland from Greenland each winter, do not follow the ups and downs of the ptarmigan population as do the gray Icelandic Gyrfalcons. Apparently, on their breeding grounds in Greenland, the resident Gyrfalcons' population cycles are tied more to the cycles of other species, such as lemmings, which are absent in Iceland.

Each year, after completing his late-June banding trip in northeastern Iceland, Olafur returns in late August to see how many young Gyrfalcons have fledged and are hunting in the nesting territories. He comes again in winter to trap and band ptarmigans near these areas. His ptarmigan studies are actually now funding his Gyrfalcon research. Money is easier to raise for ptarmigan study because they are popular gamebirds. It's important to be able to track the rise and fall of ptarmigan numbers to determine the effects of hunting—both by human and natural predators. Icelandic hunters take a considerable toll on Rock Ptarmigans, at an individual hunter level. Unlike hunters in the United States, who have strict limits on the number of birds of a particular species they can take each day, Icelandic hunters face few restrictions during the legal hunting season. Some hunters shoot more than one hundred ptarmigans a day, and some kill an astounding five hundred to one thousand of them during the course of the season. Most of these birds are sold commercially. The only reason that hunting pressure from humans hasn't had a significant impact on Rock Ptarmigan numbers yet is that so few people live in Iceland. But Olafur's studies have established vital baseline data on these birds, which should enable game managers to make sure that any declines in ptarmigan numbers fit the normal up-and-down patterns to be expected in their population cycles.

We drive through rugged terrain for most of the day, across vast lava fields, following the edge of a wide glacial river. It takes hours—traveling at times as slow as one or two miles an hour—to get to each eyrie site. I feel drowsy from a lack of sleep, but each time I start to drift off, the truck slams me hard against the side window or into the seat in front of me. (I'm crammed in the backseat of a small extended-cab pickup.) A British birder who was leading a tour group once asked Olafur for directions on how to drive across the lava field we're on now. When he returned a few days later, the man snapped: "In Britain they wouldn't let us walk on a trail like that, much less drive."

We stop to watch a Gyrfalcon eyrie in a hole in a huge cliff face, the other side of the river from us. The nest would be impossible to reach, even if we could get above it, so we gaze at the birds with a spotting scope. The adult female is completely oblivious to us, feeding her two downy chicks as we watch. Continuing along the river, we hear the roar of a huge waterfall, but it's so overcast we can barely see it. Photography is hopeless. A couple of hours later we get to a Gyrfalcon eyrie on our side of the river—and this time, for once, it's on an easy walk-in ledge. Olafur bands two young falcons, about three weeks old, as I snap some pictures using an electronic flash to compensate for the lack of sunlight. We drive through several streams along the way, where Olafur tells us horror stories of people—mostly foreigners—who have met disaster trying to ford these streams. Here's the place where a few years ago a car washed away, carrying four Japanese geologists to their deaths: They had tried to cross the river in the late afternoon on a warm day when the melting glacier produced a much greater water flow than usual. And here's where a German photographer barely escaped the same fate by climbing through the window of his small rental car and onto its roof as it sped downstream, jumping to dry ground just before it crashed over a waterfall.

We finally come to a beautiful canyon. Olafur tells us that we should climb to the top of the cliff on our side of the gorge and hike several miles upstream, searching for a Gyrfalcon nest. He will do the same on the other side of the river—after taking off his pants and wading across yet another icy torrent. In previous years the pair usually nested at the mouth of the canyon, but there was no sign of them there this time. Before we leave, Olafur boils some water for instant coffee on a small gas stove. I watch him put heaping teaspoonfuls of dark freeze-dried coffee crystals—four, five, six spoonfuls—into each cup, stirring quickly. Making loud slurping noises to cool it as we drink, we quaff the bitter black liquid and then practically explode up the hillside, like Incas scrambling up the Andes after chewing coca leaves.

It is a killer climb just to reach the rim of the canyon (despite the coffee), and once we get there the going is not much easier—a steep slope with loose rocks all the way down to the brink of the precipice. We see cliff-nesting Pink-footed Geese and ravens as we walk several miles and, finally, a Gyrfalcon. The nest is on our side, a long way up the valley, but we can't see it. Olafur counts the young with his scope. We can't even get close to the edge of the cliff at this point because of the treacherous talus slope above it.

Exhausted, we make the long hike back to the truck. Backtracking several miles overland, we stay in a remote cabin that sheep farmers use during spring roundup. Olafur tells me that centuries ago, in Iceland's early settlement period, a bustling village thrived here, not far from the seething geothermal pit that still smokes near the cabin, but I can't see any trace of the former occupants of this isolated valley. I look at my notes from the day. Going nearly constantly from early morning to past midnight, we have visited four eyries, but we only climbed to one nest and banded two birds. The others were inaccessible.

In the morning we drive to a long rift valley with massive fissures cutting deeply into the ground. I photograph a Common Raven nest with two nearly grown young and a Gyrfalcon nest with three live young and a dead one lying directly beneath the cliff in a snowbank. Though it looks fresh, the tiny nestling was a day old at best when it died; the other young are three weeks old.

Hours later, back at the truck, we drive farther south, then to another nest cliff after a lengthy cross-country drive over lush heathland. I photograph European Golden-Plovers, some with newly hatched chicks. I also take pictures of some female Rock Ptarmigans. The males I've seen so far have been too spooky to photograph. We band two more Gyrfalcon chicks and then head for the coast, where we camp out on some broad sand flats near the sea. Before we turn in for the night, we walk to a nearby Great Skua colony that Olafur needs to check as part of another study. The birds are huge—about the size of Red-tailed Hawks—and amazingly aggressive. They attack us ferociously. I hold a stick above my head to fend them off, but still they come, sounding like howitzer shells whizzing inches from my head as they brush past. Some of them dive directly at me, looking me right in the eye without flinching or veering away as I wave my stick.

This is the most intense and draining day so far. Maybe it's the combined fatigue of the entire trip catching up with us. Maybe it's because we attempt to accomplish so much. We climb to eyrie after eyrie, banding falcon after falcon, as the weather turns worse and worse. As a freezing wind and a shroud of fog move across a mountain we're climbing, I see the cliff looming high at the top. I'm amazed how far up it is, but as we reach what I think is the crest, I see that I'm mistaken. Another massive cliff rises in front of us, forming a great natural amphitheater on top of the mountain. As I hurry after Olafur and Dany, racing along fifty yards in front of me, I feel like a tired Sherpa, struggling with the weight of my camera gear, trying to follow Hillary and Tenzing as they near the top of Everest. I stop and take a quick picture of the two men disappearing into the fog near the summit. Visibility is decreasing by the minute. This is the biggest cliff we've seen yet. Although the two-hundred-yard-long rope reaches the bottom, the hundred-yard-long safety line doesn't even come close. Olafur will have to unsnap the safety line from his belt and go the last eighty feet or so using the climbing rope alone.

I don't like it. Maybe I'm more paranoid than most climbers, but I once took a bad fall at a Prairie Falcon eyrie in California. Though I didn't suffer any permanent injuries, the force of my head hitting a rock broke my climbing helmet. I later gave the helmet to the climbing-shop owner (appropriately named Cliff) whom I had bought it from, and he displayed it proudly for years, bragging: "This helmet saved a guy's life." For a long time after, I would wake in terror, dreaming I was falling off a horrendous cliff. Anyway, although it took place more than twenty years ago, this experience has made me an ultra-cautious climber. And now I feel uneasy about the climb Olafur is about to make.

Olafur ties a woven nylon belt around a huge boulder and attaches the main climbing rope and the safety rope to it on two separate carabiners. He tells Dany to pay out the safety rope slowly as he goes down, but to stop when he gets to the nest ledge—which runs for nearly forty feet along the cliff face. He'll have to unsnap the safety rope, crawl along the ledge to the birds, band them, then go back and reattach the safety rope. From there he'll go to another ledge farther down the cliff and stop to take off the safety rope again. It won't reach any farther. I am to station myself across the amphitheater from Olafur to relay messages to Dany.

Before going over the cliff, Olafur says solemnly: "If the main rope gets cut by a sharp rock on the way down, Dany, try to hold me on the safety line until Tim can come around and tie the rope off shorter. I'm taking ascenders with me, and I'll use them to try to climb back up to the top."

"How will we know if the rope gets cut?" asks Dany.

"You'll know," says Olafur. With that, he backs off the cliff into the fog and is gone. I go back to my station and wait. Visibility is getting worse and worse and the weather is getting chillier. I snap a few pictures as Olafur glides silently down the rope and the patchy fog moves in and out. He manages to band two of the three young birds, but the other one has moved so far away along the ledge that Olafur decides not to chase it. It's not worth risking his own life or that of the young falcons to band it. When I see Olafur reach the bottom of the cliff, I take a deep breath and exhale slowly, leaning back against a boulder.

It has rained all night and is still overcast, though there is no rain now. We leave our camp area and drive to another eyrie, this one on a massive cliff beside a road. Olafur and Dany drop me off at the base of the cliff so that I can point out the exact location of the nest ledge when they get to the top. It's a spectacular cliff. The safety line, again, will be far too short. You'd think that a safety line as long as a football field would be enough to reach the bottom of most eyrie cliffs, but it's definitely not in this case. Olafur and Dany drive several miles to an area where the cliff is easier to scale and hike to the stretch above where I'm waiting. It takes a couple of hours, during which time I take some telephoto shots of the falcon returning with food to feed her young. The nest is so high up the cliff that the birds are small in my viewfinder, even though I'm using a 500mm lens. It's the best I can do. I shoot a few frames of her. She doesn't seem disturbed.

Olafur finally appears above me. He looks about the size of a sparrow at the top of this precipice. I stand even with the nest ledge and point to it for him. A few minutes later he begins his descent. Some people stop on the road to see what's happening. In one car several pairs of compact binoculars peer out of the windows at the cliff, then at me, then back at the cliff. One man calls out to me in Icelandic. "Blah, blah, blah, blah?" he asks, pointing upward at Olafur. "*Falki*," I say, using my only Icelandic word. The man nods. "Blah, blah, blah, blah, yow."

Then someone else appears, a youngish man carrying a child—perhaps a year and a half old and bundled up so tightly I can't tell if it's a boy or a girl. He points at the tiny man dangling on a rope high above us and says to the child, "Blah, blah, blah, blah, Olí Nielsen." I find out later that he is one of Olafur's former field assistants, now a local schoolteacher.

After finishing with the birds, Olafur kicks off from the cliff and rappels to the ground in four or five huge bounds. Helping him with his equipment, I brush against the metal figure eight on his climbing belt that the rope runs through; it is so hot it almost blisters my hand.

It's the last day of our trip and things are winding down. In the morning we visit a spectacular eyrie on the rim of an ancient volcano. It feels like we're on top of the world here. For the first time on this trip, the sky is clear and I can view (and photograph) an immense Icelandic vista. Olafur tells me there's a legend about the lake in the caldera of this volcano. A magical horse called Nykur supposedly lives here. According to legend, she entices men to ride on her back and then takes them to the depths of the water, where they drown. The only escape is to speak the horse's name softly to her. We spend a couple of hours here, scaling the cliff and banding the young. I photograph the adult Gyrfalcons in flight and also take some pictures of Merlins at a nearby nest, farther along the rim of the volcano.

We visit one more eyrie as we make our way overland toward Akureyri. This one is across a river from us. The day is turning foggy again and it's difficult to count the nest's contents. We see at least one three-week-old falcon, but it looks like there may be more. We spend half an hour peering through the spotting scope and finally count three in all.

We stop at a great waterfall called Godafoss—Falls of the Gods—the place where Þorgeir the Lawgiver, in A.D. 999, tossed the old wooden Nordic idols over the falls and declared that Iceland would henceforth be a Christian nation. We sit at a small picnic table near the falls, shivering in the icy breeze as we wolf down sardine-and-cheese sandwiches and guzzle bad instant coffee. It's really over now, and we're all physically spent. We look like hell. I have a two-week beard and have probably lost ten pounds. And I'm filthy. In a few hours we'll be flying back to Reykjavik, and at midday tomorrow I'll be on my way back to New York. It's been an amazing journey. Together we have visited twenty-seven eyries, climbed to eighteen of them, and banded fifty-two young Gyrfalcons—definitely a respectable showing.

As I think back on Olafur, jotting down his copious notes below yet another Gyrfalcon eyrie, I see how well this fits the pattern of his countrymen. Icelanders are inveterate note takers. Since the dawn of their country, more than one thousand years ago, they've recorded all the interesting aspects of their national life in minute detail in various sagas dating from their early settlement days. Nothing is forgotten here. As we traveled the back roads (if you could call them roads) of Iceland, Olafur told us all the local gossip and lore of each area—bouncing easily from Viking times to the present and back again. Here's the cave where the outlaw Grettir the Strong hid centuries ago. Here's the Gyrfalcon eyrie where Hermann Göring's men came to take young falcons. Here's the river ford where the Japanese geologists met their fate. It's all there: remembered in the oral and written traditions of the people, to be spoken of for centuries—along with tales about the itinerant ornithologist from Reykjavik who traveled these rocky roads for decades in the late twentieth and early twenty-first centuries, in search of the *falki*.

2

TRUE NORTH

July 1999

Thule Air Base in northern Greenland is an eerie place. With its huge fuel tanks, its rows of long barracks raised above ground and weighted down with massive concrete blocks to withstand hurricane-force winds, and its elaborate network of heating pipes threading across, around, and into every building, the place looks like a NASA outpost on Mars. And the barren, reddish hills and vast glacier looming above only add to the effect. Still, it's a welcome sight after flying due north for six hours in the cramped rear cabin of a cargo plane with nothing below but glaciers, icebergs, and dark, frigid sea as far as you can see.

It's late July, shortly after the annual breakup of the pack ice in northwestern Greenland, and I've come to visit the High Arctic Institute—a private research center headquartered at the base. The Peregrine Fund launched the institute several years ago and is conducting ongoing studies of far northern birds. I'm traveling with Bill Burnham, president of The Peregrine Fund, and we plan to spend a couple of weeks banding Dovekies and exploring the coast and offshore islands of Greenland, searching for nesting Gyrfalcons and Peregrine Falcons.

At a latitude of 76 degrees, 32 minutes north, Thule is hundreds of miles north of the Arctic Circle and only about eight hundred miles from the North Pole. At this time of year the sun is up twenty-four hours a day and doesn't even touch the hilltops as it makes its daily circuit around the sky. It can be as bright at midnight as it is at noon. But in October the sun sets for the winter, plunging the area into darkness until April. The winds here are legendary. The enormous fuel tanks at the front of the base—as large as those in an oil refinery—bear massive dents from the incredible pounding of the northern Greenland winds, which can hit at any season, bringing all travel to a halt. On several occasions Bill has been stuck far from the base for days at a time—hunkered in a low tent in the lee of some protective boulders, waiting for the squall to die down.

More frightening was the time two years ago when Bill, his son Kurt, and Jack Stephens (the base's weather forecaster) made a horrendous voyage in a twin-engine rubber boat, traveling from their Dovekie base camp south of Thule up the coast during a storm. As they plied their way northward, the seas churned violently and the winds blew at more than one hundred miles per hour, pushing apartment-house-sized icebergs shoreward. With icebergs moving fast behind them, they ran the boat up a glacial stream at Cape Atholl and tied off on some boulders, just before the icebergs clogged the entrance. If they had arrived just five minutes later, the stream would have been blocked, and they would have had to make an all-out run north, around the point and into Wolstenholme Fjord to reach Thule. Bill doubts they would have made it. As they came in to land, the snow was blowing horizontally, drifting several feet deep in places. And this was on August 8—the height of summer in northern Greenland. Everyone who travels by boat in this area constantly searches for inlets, bays, or other sheltered areas to run to if a storm comes up, because the weather can change in a matter of minutes.

On our third day in Greenland we get up at 4 A.M., eat a quick breakfast, and head to sea. We've been grounded at the base by gale-force winds for the past thirty hours but are heading to the Dovekie base camp today, hoping that the weather conditions will continue to improve. Bill and I travel in the red boat, while Kurt and Jack take the faster gray one. These are both Zodiac-style rubber boats, although they carry the brand name Achilles—which makes me wonder what their Achilles' heel might be. They each run two hearty forty-horsepower outboard engines, which provide power and dependability: If one engine dies at an inopportune moment, you still have the second engine to get you safely home.

The temperature plummets as soon as we leave shore and start threading through the icebergs in Wolstenholme Fjord, a large inlet, miles across, leading from Thule Air Base at North Star Bay to the open sea. Even though I'm wearing an expedition-grade parka, I'm unbearably cold a lot of the time. I put on a fleece hat, pull my head deep inside my parka hood, and cover my eyes with glacier glasses to block the icy wind. I only wish I had something to cover my nose, which feels like a block of ice stuck to the middle of my face.

Though the environment here is harsh, it is incredibly rich. Everywhere I look I see bird life—squadrons of Common Eiders fly past constantly; Black Guillemots, Thick-billed Murres, and Dovekies skitter over the frigid water in front of us.

Two days earlier we took a shakedown cruise to make sure the boats were running well, and we visited many of the bird islands in Wolstenholme Fjord. On Dalrymple Rock, a pointed outcropping about fifteen miles from the base, we visited nesting colonies of Atlantic Puffins, Common Eiders, and Black Guillemots. I took many full-frame pictures of these birds as I scrambled around a rocky cliff with my cumbersome 500mm lens and tripod. We also explored Saunder's Island, the largest island by far in the area. The cliffs surrounding the island are full of nesting Thick-billed Murres, which is not surprising—the Inuit name for the island, Agpat, means "murre." We circled the island, checking the lofty sea cliffs for falcon nests but found none, although we did find many nesting Black-legged Kittiwakes and Glaucous Gulls in addition to the murres.

As soon as we round the point and move into the open sea, we're hit by large swells that pound the boats, rocking the icebergs around us. But at least we can see the big bergs. It's the smaller, low-lying chunks of ice you have to scan for constantly—especially the clear ones that lie on the surface of the water like great sheets of Saran Wrap but can slice a rubber boat like a can opener or flip it over, spilling its passengers into the icy sea. It takes only a few minutes to lose consciousness and die in this frigid water. Even Inuit walrus hunters, who know these waters better than anyone, sometimes wash ashore, perhaps tossed from their boats by hidden chunks of ice or waves. Most of the local people don't even wear life preservers. They call them "body finders," which is about all they're good for if you fall overboard.

When we reach our base camp, several miles south of Cape Atholl, we take the boats up a glacial river and tie them to boulders. It is high tide but in a few hours the tide will go out, leaving the boats grounded until the tide comes in again. It's vital to have a tide chart and follow the risings and fallings of the tides closely; otherwise you could get stuck for hours before the tide comes up enough to float your boat.

Unloading the boats resembles a military assault. We form a line, handing trapping gear, tents, stoves, food, and other equipment from person to person, quickly emptying the craft. We then clamber over the streamside rocks and carry everything up a steep trail to a large, grassy, plateaulike shelf fifty or sixty feet above the river, where we pitch our tents.

This is an ideal campsite, close to a major Dovekie colony and with a spectacular view of the sea and a convenient supply of fresh water at the stream. But we're not the first people to camp at this remote spot. Close to where we pitch our tents are traces of an ancient Inuit encampment—the foundations of several huts dug into the ground. After Bill first reported seeing these ruins, a team of Danish archaeologists visited the site and said they were centuries old, perhaps the oldest ruins of their kind in northern Greenland. These eight-by-ten-foot huts probably originally had whalebone struts holding up a roof of animal skins, and each one would have housed an entire family. The Inuit no doubt came here to catch Dovekies, which to this day they consider a great delicacy. They traditionally caught the birds by snatching them out of the air, midflight, using a hoop net on the end of a long narwhal tusk.

The Dovekie colony lies straight across the river from us, up a steep grassy slope, among the talus rock at the base of a cliff. Peregrine Fund researchers have been trapping and banding Dovekies here for the past five summers. We set up mist nets in three areas of the colony, right at the base of the talus slope. Each year the team has set up the nets in exactly the same places. The researchers are trying to learn more about the nest-site fidelity of these birds as well as their longevity. Not much is currently known about Dovekies, and virtually all of the data the institute gathers is useful. The birds fly far out to sea to feed. When they return to their nests, their gular pouches are bulging with slimy, purplish red zooplankton, which they regurgitate for their young. They are sociable birds, frequently gathering in little groups, chattering softly and interacting with each other. Though they are not much bigger than starlings, they remind me of penguins as they waddle around together, showing off their striking black-and-white plumages.

Each of us lay on the grassy slope below the mist nets, hiding under see-through camouflage material, waiting for Dovekies to get snagged. The trapping is sporadic at best. Sometimes an hour or more goes by with no action, and then suddenly five or six birds fly into the nets at once. Some of the Dovekies immediately spin around when caught and require a lot of work to untangle. They nip our fingers hard with their little puffinlike bills but usually don't quite break the skin.

Lone Glaucous Gulls occasionally cruise over the colony, flushing thousands of screaming Dovekies, which fly around above the canyon in a panic until the danger passes. The sound is deafening but oddly familiar, like the crowd roar at a major-league baseball stadium when a home team player hits a grand slam, but heard from five miles away. I see a Glaucous Gull fly past with a Dovekie in its bill, once again putting up countless scores of birds. I also spot an arctic fox working the colony, sniffing around, trying to find an adult Dovekie or a chick sitting a little too close to the entrance of its nest hole in the pile of talus rubble.

We quit trapping at seven in the evening. The sun has barely broken through the bone-chilling fog all day. Kurt cooks a spaghetti dinner with meat sauce, vegetables, and home-baked biscuits. It's the best-tasting meal I've ever eaten—except for the wine. The chardonnay Bill and I brought from Thule has turned an odd pinkish red color, somewhat like the color of gasoline, and it smells like vinegar. Was it shaken up too much as we bucked the waves coming here? Is this what they mean by bruising the wine? I don't know. We drink it anyway.

This is the third day of Dovekie trapping for Bill and me. Jack and Kurt returned to Thule yesterday so that Kurt could give a talk about the High Arctic Institute. He was also going to pick up another researcher, Jim Enderson, at the airport. We catch several more Dovekies in the morning but things are definitely slowing down. At one point Bill shows me a banded Dovekie he retrapped. The band, provided by the Danish government, is numbered 001— the first Dovekie that Bill banded here when the study began five years earlier. "These birds are living longer than many people thought," he tells me. The site fidelity of these birds is also amazing. All of the retraps from year to year tend to occur in exactly the same section of cliff where they were originally trapped.

Bill plans to continue banding Dovekies in this location in the years ahead. He sees Dovekies as an effective barometer for monitoring the health of the High Arctic maritime ecosystem. In many ways zooplankton and the animals that consume it are the keys to the whole food chain here. Dovekies exist entirely on zooplankton from the deep Arctic seas. Many predatory birds and mammals in turn depend on the easy-to-catch Dovekies for food. If global warming, environmental contamination, or other ecological threats should devastate the zooplankton in the High Arctic, a crash in Dovekie numbers might be the first indication of a problem.

Although Bill has been a raptor researcher for most of his adult life, he is clearly fascinated by Dovekies. "The site fidelity of these birds is so phenomenal that you could probably learn enough from a small population like this one to extrapolate the data to the entire population." Dovekies nest on newly fallen rock talus slopes and breed there each summer until the slopes become lichen covered and the rocks start to break down. Then they leave to find new nesting areas in places that have had recent rockslides. Dovekies provide food for more than just the animals that prey on them. The grass and peat at the base of these cliffs are there only because of the guano these birds excrete, providing a rich source of nitrogen for plants. Musk oxen, arctic hares, and other herbivores make good use of the habitat created by the Dovekies as they transform zooplankton from the deep sea into rich green grass on the hillsides.

It has been foggy most of the morning, but the mist starts to lift at midday, about the time we are leaving. The tide is turning just as we pull out. Bill says if we'd left five minutes later as the tide was rushing out, the boat would've been stuck. We would have had to unload it quickly, push it into deeper water, then load it all over again. We cruise up the coast in the eerie sunlight, stopping at the Cape Atholl Gyrfalcon nest. We spot the adults on a nearby cliff face—the male sitting several feet below the female. These are the first nesting white Gyrfalcons I've ever seen. They are amazingly pale. I can't see a dark mark on the adult male's entire body.

We tie the boat to a boulder at the bottom of a massive sea cliff. The nest must be a good six hundred feet up and a tough climb. I almost leave my camera gear on the boat rather than taking it on such a treacherous climb. But then I think: When else will I get a chance to photograph white Gyrfalcons?

It's a struggle trying to keep up with Bill, who climbs like a mountain goat, consistently staying twenty or thirty feet above me. What a climb. It seems to get steeper and steeper. And now we're not even climbing on solid rock but reaching high over our heads to grasp round tussocks of grass, which we're using for handholds and footholds—and we're not using any ropes, ascenders, or pitons to assist us.

About two-thirds of the way up Bill stops to wait for me and offers to carry my gear for a while. Of course, I have something to prove and don't want to seem like a wimp, so I wait a full tenth of a second before replying, "Yes!" I feel guilty but grateful. We climb to a ledge directly even with the nest, across a narrow gully. The view is fantastic, and a beautiful, fully feathered young white Gyrfalcon sits sunning himself at the front of the nest ledge. I take many pictures of him and also some of a Glaucous Gull with one young on another ledge.

As we sit watching the young falcon, fog starts drifting in again. Bill suggests we make our way back to the boat as soon as possible. It is even more treacherous on the way down than it was going up. I try descending by a different route than Bill, hoping it's easier, but I end up standing on a lone boulder, far below, with waves lapping against it. Bill finally drives around with the boat and I jump aboard.

It is flat calm and eerily quiet on the way back, with none of the tossing swells we had on the trip in here three days earlier. But the fog continues to build, coming on thick and heavy and gray. Massive white icebergs loom ahead. The thunder of calving glaciers echoes in the distance. Some of these glaciers move more than a hundred feet a day and calve icebergs the size of city blocks. We move slowly along, trying to keep sight of shore without hitting rocks jutting from the water. At one place, near a river delta, the water is only two feet deep and we have to crawl along, searching for protruding boulders and jagged ice. It is freezing all the way back. I hunker into my parka, the hood pulled tight. My thoughts are far away. The endless drone of the engines sounds like the chant echoing from a distant Buddhist monastery.

Through the fog I make out the indistinct shapes of some shacks that the Inuit use as a winter hunting camp. It occurs to me what a fleeting presence the Native People have been for me here, more intuitively sensed than seen. I've run across signs of them everywhere—their piled rock graves on the islands; their food caches of walrus carcasses and eider eggs buried in the shallow, perpetually cool beach gravel—but I've met few of them. I remember seeing an Inuit hunter's motorboat tied to the jetty in North Star Bay. The boat's small outboard engine was bare to the elements and rusted, its metal cover long since lost. Three huge plastic containers of fuel, a couple of duffel bags, and several cases of Pepsi-Cola were the only supplies aboard. A high-caliber bolt-action rifle lay on top, in plain sight and badly rusted. But lashed on top of the boat and to one side, to leave room for the boat's driver, sat a sleek Inuit kayak, the most beautiful, well-crafted one I've ever seen, with a handheld harpoon attached to it. What an odd mix of cultures and technologies was represented there.

It is foggy today, so we take the opportunity to work on the boats, making minor adjustments. We eat at the mess hall, which is an interesting place. In large, bold letters on the wall as you enter is a message written in both English and Danish warning about the dangers of eating high-cholesterol foods. This is much like the health warning on the side of a pack of cigarettes, because the food they're serving is an amazing assemblage of greasy bacon, ham, and fried eggs, as well as wonderful, butter-rich Danish rolls. As I stand in the cafeteria line, a young Danish woman behind the counter asks me if I'd like some bacon. "Yes, please, a couple of pieces," I tell her. She reaches into the huge pile of bacon with tongs and pulls out fifteen or twenty thick slices, stuck together like glue. Dropping them on my plate, she smiles and says, "I hope you like bacon."

Thule Air Base is like a huge life-support system dropped in the middle of a wilderness. Walk just a mile or so from the base and you're in a different world—one of the most unforgiving environments on the planet. Few roads exist up here—just the gravel road that runs five or six miles to the Ballistic Missile Early Warning System facility and a much longer road, which is rarely passable anymore, that leads to an abandoned loran station at Cape Atholl—so boats are the preferred means of travel for the researchers working here.

In its Cold War heyday Thule Air Base employed several thousand military and civilian personnel. Bombers armed with nuclear weapons flew constantly, while others stood by in secret hangars as a deterrent to attacks by Soviet bombers coming over the Arctic Ocean. But satellite technology and guided missiles have made this base less important than it was in the past, and its footprint has been shrinking each year as staff is moved out and barracks are demolished.

The High Arctic Institute is headquartered in a barracks that would probably have been demolished if The Peregrine Fund hadn't acquired it. And it's a wonderful place—warm, dry, and homey. When you push down the lever locking the eight-inch-thick front door, which resembles the door of a bank vault, you're about as protected from the elements as you can get at this frozen northern latitude.

In the afternoon Bill and I climb Dundas Mountain to look for the pair of Peregrine Falcons that nests there each summer. For several years this site has been regarded as the northernmost Peregrine Falcon nest in the Western Hemisphere and perhaps the world (though a few days later, in an exploratory trip north to Booth Sound, we find three more Peregrine Falcon nests that beat this latitude record). We climb up the backside of the rock while Jack and Kurt and Jim Enderson take the boat around front, along the cliffs, to see if they can spot the nest from below.

Dundas Mountain is a huge butte rising one thousand feet above North Star Bay and is Thule Air Base's most distinctive landmark. It's also another steep, tough climb on broken, loose, jagged rock. (This time, though, I manage to carry my camera gear all the way myself.) We walk around the entire top of Dundas Mountain and finally flush both birds on the air-base side. I take some shots of the falcons flying over the iceberg-filled water, but we don't stay long—peregrines nest much later than Gyrfalcons, and these birds probably have small young. We don't want to keep them off their nest long.

I photograph an ancient Inuit fertility statue—a huge, headless, limbless female torso carved of stone that faces toward the open sea. I also photograph a memorial cairn for Knud Rasmussen erected on top of Dundas Mountain. In 1910 Rasmussen and his friend Peter Freuchen founded the trading post and village of Thule at the base of the mountain. The two of them were major Arctic explorers, traveling by dogsled across the northernmost parts of Greenland and extending Danish rule to the entire area. Both men married Inuit women and lived most of their lives in Greenland.

Later I visit their village, which has changed little since they lived here, except that it is now a ghost town. When Thule Air Base was constructed in the early 1950s, the Danes built a new village for the Inuit and other inhabitants about a hundred miles north of here and moved them. This is an amazing place—so silent and peaceful that you'd never know there's an air base just on the other side of Dundas Mountain. In the shadow of the neat frame houses lie traces of earlier humans: earthworks and the foundations of sod huts. Here on the shores of North Star Bay a human community thrived for centuries. And here, too, the great Robert Peary anchored many times on his Arctic explorations. Though history has been unkind to him, even questioning his greatest achievement of reaching the North Pole and condemning him for exploiting the Inuit, it is he more than most of the other explorers who has the respect of these people. He adopted their ways and used their techniques to succeed as an explorer.

As I stand in the purple hue of a late-summer night in the High Arctic of Greenland, I can't help thinking about the Inuit who once lived here, as well as Peary, Rasmussen, Freuchen, and all the other people from faraway lands who have been drawn to Greenland, again and again and again, as though addicted to the place. And I realize that this also applies to my friends at the High Arctic Institute—including Jack Stephens, who has lived at Thule Air

Base for twenty-seven years. Jack, an affable, good-natured Georgian, had been recently divorced and was living in Arizona when he saw an ad for the position of base weather forecaster. He jumped at the chance to come here and has never even thought about returning to a stateside job. An avid wildlife photographer, Jack takes a leave each summer to work with Peregrine Fund researchers, accompanying them on all their explorations. In winter he lives alone at the High Arctic Institute, surrounded by his library-sized collection of books—ranging in topics from history and science to literature and the arts—and his impressive collection of classical music CDs.

Then there's Kurt Burnham, who, though only twenty-three years old, has spent nine summers in Greenland. Earlier this year he made a two-hundred-mile journey by dogsled with an Inuit, searching for new Gyrfalcon nesting areas. The temperature hovered in the fifty-below-zero range the entire time. He told me that his goal is to someday go to the North Pole by dogsled, as Peary did nearly a century earlier.

And finally there's Bill Burnham, one of the most determined people I've ever met. Several days after we climb Dundas Mountain he goes back alone, carrying all the climbing gear with him. As he reaches the top of the cliff, Jim Enderson and I stand on the nearby pier at Thule Air Base, peering at the cliff with a spotting scope and talking with Bill via walkie-talkie, trying to help him locate the nest site. As I watch, he climbs down the cliff and back up again three times before finding the right ledge. Each climb is well over a hundred feet, and he does it quickly to minimize any bother to the birds.

A couple of weeks later, in Boise, Idaho, I speak with Bill Mattox, president of the Conservation Research Foundation, who had sent Bill Burnham on his first trip to Greenland in the early 1970s. (Mattox himself had first gone to Greenland in 1951 and had met Peter Freuchen.) He laughs when I tell him how hard it was to keep up with Bill as we hiked overland or climbed cliffs. "Bill was always a real tundra burner," he says. As they were crossing massive expanses of Greenland tundra, he tells me, Burnham would consistently walk a hundred yards or more ahead and then stop, sit on a rock, and wait for Mattox to catch up. "As soon as I got there, he'd stand up and say, 'Well, we better get going now,'" he adds, laughing.

Later in our conversation Mattox gives me a knowing look and says, "You've got the bug; you'll go back to Greenland."

Could be.

3

GREENLAND
DIARY

July 2000

> *The five essays in "Greenland Diary" first appeared in the online magazine*
> Slate. *Each week* Slate's *"Diary" column features a different writer, chroni-*
> *cling an interesting five-day period in his or her life. I had to write a seven-*
> *hundred-word essay every day from July 10 through July 14, 2000, while*
> *traveling in Greenland—and then figure out how to get it to the Slate editor-*
> *ial offices in Seattle. The pieces were posted on the Web almost in real time, a*
> *few hours after I sent them via e-mail.*

Posted: Monday, July 10, 2000, 10:30 A.M. Pacific time. Well, I'm on my way . . . again. Greenland, the sequel. Back to the frigid water that freezes on your parka whenever a wave splashes over the boat hull, the apartment-house-sized icebergs that rock precariously as you motor past, and the colossal cliffs rising one thousand feet or more out of the sea—the cliffs you have to climb to reach the nesting falcons. I'm en route to join an expedition in progress—a thousand-plus-mile boat trip up the western coast of Greenland to study Peregrine Falcons, Gyrfalcons, and various seabirds. The other people on the team left two weeks ago, and I have to hook up with them at Uummannaq, a small town midway up the coast. I'll be in Greenland for three weeks, covering the trip for *Living Bird* magazine.

In case you don't know much about Greenland, it's that huge mass of ice you fly across when you're taking the polar route to or from Europe. At 1.8 million square kilometers in size, it has the distinction of being the largest island in the world—not counting the island continent of Australia—and is also the northernmost country. Most of Greenland lies above the Arctic Circle, and it served as the base from which Robert Peary and several other polar explorers launched their attempts to reach the North Pole, just a few hundred miles farther north. But you get the picture. It's a cold place—winter or summer. Only fifty-five thousand people live there, mostly in the south, and the capital "city" of Nuuk boasts only fourteen thousand residents—barely a village in U.S. terms. Walk out of almost any town, settlement, or military base in Greenland and you're in a howling wilderness within minutes.

As always when you go to Greenland, you have to take the trip in stages. Today my wife is driving me from Ithaca, New York, to Ottawa, Ontario (about a five-hour trip), where I'll spend the night and catch an early-morning flight with a tiny Canadian airline that specializes in taking the Inuit and other northern dwellers or workers from one part of the Arctic to another. The destinations have difficult-to-spell (and pronounce) names like Kuujjuaq, Iqaluit, and Nuuk. I'll fly first to Baffin Island, then continue on to Kangerlussuaq, Greenland, where I'll probably have to take a series of domestic flights on small planes or helicopters to reach Uummannaq. Someone is supposed to meet me in Kangerlussuaq and fill me in on the details. (I imagine myself, like Jim Phelps in the old TV show *Mission: Impossible*, being handed a tape that self-destructs after I listen to it.)

At least I know what I'm getting into this year. I was clueless a year ago when I went to cover a Peregrine Fund research project in northwestern

Greenland. In the weeks before that trip I kept calling Bill Burnham—president of The Peregrine Fund—trying to make sure I had everything I'd need. Now, Bill is the quintessential stoical westerner, a man who doesn't waste words on idle chatter, so you tend to listen closely when he speaks. Our phone calls often had an unnerving effect on me. As soon as I hung up, I'd usually call a mail-order outfitter right away and buy more gear. One day Bill casually told me that I'd need an all-season tent that could withstand 125-mile-an-hour winds.

"Sometimes these Arctic storms come up without warning, blowing snow sideways, even in summer," he said. "You might have to hunker down in your tent behind some boulders for a few days until it passes."

"Right," I said. "No problem." I was trembling as I called the outfitter to order a top-of-the-line four-season tent. Then, the next time we talked, Bill said (with a deadpan Clint Eastwood delivery), "You know, a person could die out there—*r-e-a-l e-e-z-e-e*." I went right out and bought a new goose-down sleeping bag, an expedition-grade parka, moleskin long underwear, weatherproof gloves, fleece glove liners, and a pile of arctic socks. And whenever my wife complained about the hundreds of dollars I was blowing on this stuff, I'd tell her: "You know, a person could die out there—*r-e-a-l e-e-z-e-e*."

And then I got there, and soon we were cruising through ice floes in the fog near Cape Atholl, trying to avoid hitting patches of clear ice that hung in the water, ready to slice our inflated rubber boats. The brand name of the boats we were using, Achilles, did nothing to inspire confidence in me.

But things are looking up this year. The Peregrine Fund has a new, supposedly unsinkable boat we'll be using on the trip. Its brand name: Safe Boat.

Posted: Tuesday, July 11, 2000, 10 A.M. Pacific time. I got a strange e-mail message last night from the person arranging my travel in Greenland. He said someone from KISS would meet me when my plane landed in Kangerlussuaq, Greenland. For a second I had visions of someone from the rock band Kiss rushing up to the gangway, clad in black leather and white face paint with tongue flickering snakelike. But no. It turns out there's a facility called the

Kangerlussuaq International Science Support that houses researchers who visit the area. Now I have to wonder: Is KISS an acronym they created deliberately (and if so, why?) or was it just a coincidence? Anyway, I'll be staying at KISS overnight, then taking another flight in the morning.

As I sit here in the Ottawa airport, I feel sick in the pit of my stomach. I just said good-bye to my wife, Rachel, and two of my kids (Clara, seven, and Gwendolyn, nine months), who came to see me off. And now I'm alone, and the plane's not leaving for a couple of hours. I hope I have a better time with this airline than I had last year with the military transport company that flew me from Baltimore to Thule Air Base in northwestern Greenland. That airline was a real low-bidder operation with an aging fleet of 1960s-vintage DC-8 transport planes that fly once a week to odd places like Saudi Arabia or Greenland. These planes have no windows or seats in the forward 80 percent of the cabin—just row upon row of pallets, lashed firmly to the deck, carrying vital military equipment such as toilet paper and beer. The twenty or so passengers—made up of airmen and civilian contractors (and falcon researchers)—were all stuck in the tiny rear tail section. I remember reading the rules printed on the back of the "orders" I'd been issued allowing me to fly to the air base: special restrictions on the type and the amount of various firearms and ordnance you could carry aboard as hand luggage.

Our plane was due to leave at two o'clock in the morning. We didn't load up until four. Some of the civilian contractors flying with us were in bad shape from drinking all night. One young guy with a serious fear of flying was semi-comatose, sprawled in his seat with his mouth agape; apparently he'd taken a high dose of tranquilizers, hoping to sleep through the flight.

Well, we didn't leave that night. After we sweated through a couple of hours in the muggy cabin, the captain said the plane was unsafe and would be grounded for twenty-four hours. It was 9 A.M. by the time they'd bused us to a hotel thirty miles away. (They had to carry out the guy who took the tranquilizers.) And it was hot . . . *r-e-e-e-al* hot. And muggy. And everything I brought with me, except the now grimy and smelly polo shirt on my back, was expedition-grade Arctic-wear, good down to minus sixty degrees Fahrenheit. Even the jeans I had on were lined with Polarfleece; I figured I'd be doing all my traveling at night and stepping from the plane into, at best, twenty-five-degree temperatures with an icy wind blowing. Why waste luggage space with a bunch of warm-weather clothes?

It was ninety-eight degrees and steamy in Baltimore. As I walked out of the hotel, trying to get to the mall across the street, I was driven back by a palpable wall of heat and had to duck back inside the hotel. (Now I know what it means to sweat buckets.) I reported back to BWI airport as ordered at 2400 hours, and four hours later we were back on the plane. This time Tranquilizer Boy had held off on taking his drugs until he was positive we were taking off. He had them in his hand and was washing them down one by one with a bottle of seltzer water as we taxied across the airfield. But then I noticed that the pilot kept revving the engines in a way I'd never heard before, and, well . . . it didn't sound good. Kind of clattery or metallic. And then the pilot was on the horn scrubbing the flight for another twenty-four hours. Tranquilizer Boy was already staggering and walking into walls by the time the bus arrived to take us back to the hotel.

On day three it was still sweltering in Baltimore. By the time I was back in the airplane cabin at 0300 hours, I was drenched in sweat, smelly, and, I admit it, terrified about flying in this thing—but still not as bad off as Tranquilizer Boy, who'd downed all his pills the previous two nights and now had nothing left to take. His friends kept plying him with hits of Jack Daniels, but it seemed only to make him more nervous. This time when the pilot revved the engines, they sounded marginally better than the night before. And then we were off, rolling slowly at first . . . and then faster and faster and faster—and yet, not as fast as jets usually go. And we seemed to be going an amazingly long distance with the wheels still on the ground. Then I could see the end of the runway quickly approaching in the darkness, and I could tell the pilot was going for it, pulling up six feet, eight feet . . . and I started thinking about an article I read once about a DC-8 cargo plane full of beef cattle that crashed on takeoff in Alaska, scattering dead cows and humans over a mile-wide area. And then we were clear, with twenty feet to spare as we passed over the chain-link fence at the end of the airport. But no one clapped or cheered. We just sat in silence, gazing ahead into the darkness.

Posted: Wednesday, July 12, 2000, 10 A.M. Pacific time. Midnight; Aktivitetscenter Nordylyset; Kangerlussuaq, Greenland: Half a dozen Danes slouch at the tiny tables scattered around the dimly lit restaurant-bar, smoking cigarettes and speaking rapidly as an old disco tune bumps along in the background: "Stayin' alive, stayin' alive." Alone in the corner, on a stuffed leather sofa beneath a polar bear skin rug on one wall and a bleached-out caribou skull on the other, I nurse a full mug of Danish beer as I write.

Yes. I made it to Greenland, and I met the man from KISS: Bent Brodersen. Apparently he's the person to know around here. Like Rick in the movie *Casablanca*, he knows everyone. He can pull strings. He makes things happen. In fact, he's the one who sent me to this place for dinner. I'm afraid it's no Rick's. Besides some assorted wines and Danish beer, the menu offers pizza and several kinds of paste—which I guess is the Danish word for "pasta." I ordered the one with shrimp. Come to think of it, paste is a pretty good description of what I ate.

I'm writing this piece the old-fashioned way—in longhand, with a pencil. (Didn't Hemingway once say something to the effect that to wear out two number 2 pencils is a good day's work writing? All I can say is, he must have been sharpening his pencils with a dull hunting knife.) KISS has only one computer available for visitors to send e-mail, so I don't want to hog it.

At 1 A.M. they boot me; it's closing time. So I'm out on the street in Kangerlussuaq . . . slouching toward KISS in an icy, driving rain. Of course, this is one of those Land-of-the-Midnight-Sun kind of places, so it's almost as light now as it will be at one o'clock in the afternoon—which isn't saying much; it's been overcast and drizzly all day. But I'm here, and I've already started seeing nesting falcons. And now I'm typing away on the only available computer at KISS, and I don't care if anyone else wants to use it. I drank my one mug of Danish beer, and I'm not getting off this computer until I finish writing this damn thing. Who knows? I might be dictating my next diary entry to my wife via satellite telephone, so I want to take advantage of this opportunity to use a computer. (Hemingway can keep his damn pencils.)

I dropped in on a couple of falcon researchers—Kathryn Wightman and Gregg Doney—this afternoon as soon as I got here. They work for The Peregrine Fund each summer, monitoring nesting falcons in a one-hundred-square-mile study area near Kangerlussuaq. This is a rich area for falcons, with fourteen pairs of Gyrfalcons and probably more than a hundred pairs of peregrines. It's not an easy job. They spend weeks at a time hiking overland, camping the entire time as they check each site. But the hard work is a few weeks ahead, when the young peregrines are old enough to be banded. (They've already banded the Gyrfalcons, which nest earlier than peregrines.) The two of them and one or two other teams will band as many of the young as possible before they fledge.

The recovery rate from their peregrine banding is incredible—about 7 percent. These are either birds that have been found dead or ones trapped and then re-released by banders working along the East Coast and Gulf Coast of North America. Many have been recovered in Cuba, Central America, and South America, as far down as Argentina. An adult that nested at one of the local nests was shot last year in Bolivia.

That's one of the interesting differences between Peregrine Falcons and Gyrfalcons. The Arctic peregrines are transients, coming to Greenland for only a few short months in summer, then returning to their "real" home in Latin America. The Gyrfalcons, in contrast, tough it out year-round. They're amazing birds, far larger and more powerful than peregrines. A peregrine usually must dive from a great height to achieve the speed it needs to overtake and bind to or knock down its prey—usually a bird. But a Gyrfalcon can explode powerfully from near ground level, chasing its prey over open country for miles if necessary or high into the sky until it wears it down. But if it wants to, a Gyrfalcon can also plummet meteorlike from on high like a peregrine. They're the perfect Arctic predator. Still, it's remarkable that they can survive in such a harsh environment, where even in summer great storms can come up, with one-hundred-plus-mile-per-hour winds blowing snow across the tundra for days, making it impossible to fly, much less hunt. How can they possibly survive? Some researchers speculate that they hunker down in holes in cliffs in a semi-dormant state, waiting out the storms. I've never heard of any other raptor doing this, but it makes sense.

Gregg and Kathryn took me to three peregrine nests a short distance from Kangerlussuaq—one is on a high cliff behind the airport and another I can see through the window of my room. I could tell when I first met the two researchers that they were not eager to go out and look at falcon nests. They'd just come back from a couple of weeks in the field and were beat. But after talking with them about falcons for twenty minutes or so, we all got excited about seeing some peregrines. A few minutes later we were shivering beneath a massive cliff, looking up at a female Peregrine Falcon sitting on her nest ledge. I suppose I should be thankful that the young peregrines in the Kangerlussuaq area are still too young to band. Otherwise they might want me to climb to the top of the cliff and rappel to the nest.

I'm getting up in a couple of hours—if I ever get to sleep—and having coffee with Gregg and Kathryn. Then Bent is taking me to the airport, where I'll take a plane north to Ilulissat, then take another plane to Qaarsut, then take a helicopter to Uummannaq, and then maybe . . . someday . . . catch up with the falcon research boat before it heads north all the way to Thule.

Posted: Thursday, July 13, 2000, 10 A.M. Pacific time. True to form, it's taking longer than expected to get where I'm going in Greenland and meet the research boat. I got as far as Ilulissat yesterday morning, then I was told I'd have to wait until early this morning to continue to Uummannaq. But I made the most of the delay and spent much of the afternoon yesterday crawling over rocks and tundra to photograph Lapland Longspurs, a common songbird in the Arctic.

I also took time to drop in at the Knud Rasmussen Museum, which is in the house where the famed explorer and ethnologist grew up in the late nineteenth century. I guess it's not too much of a stretch for a bird researcher to mention Rasmussen here, since he was killed by a bird . . . sort of. Rasmussen, whose father was a Danish vicar in Ilulissat, spent most of his life with a group of Inuit in the Thule area of northwestern Greenland. Now, the Inuit love to eat Dovekies—small, puffinlike seabirds that live only in far northern waters. They take a fresh-killed seal and carefully remove its body from inside its skin, which makes a nice big bag, lined with an inch or so of blubber. Then they fill the skin completely with Dovekie carcasses. The Inuit catch these birds with nets on the end of long poles as the birds fly to and from their nest sites in rocky hillsides. And then they bury the stuffed seal in beach gravel . . . for a year or two. They'll usually pull these things out in midwinter as a special celebration, breaking the seal open with an ax and chowing down on the well-marinated but uncooked birds. Anyway, poor Knud apparently died of food poisoning in the early 1930s after eating some spoiled Dovekies.

Greenland's history is always just below the surface—literally. It's too difficult to dig deep graves in the frozen ground, so the Inuit generally just pile rocks on top of bodies to keep them safe from polar bears, sled dogs, and various other scavengers. During last year's research trip, searching for nesting falcons north of Thule, we found many traces of the Inuit—caches of walrus carcasses and eider eggs as well as piled rock graves, often with bones or bodies visible—on the islands we visited. And it's difficult to tell whether these are five years or five hundred years old, everything is so well preserved. A few years ago Peregrine Fund researchers found the foundations of several early Inuit dwellings near a Dovekie colony and alerted a Danish archaeologist. They turned out to be among the earliest human dwellings yet discovered in northern Greenland.

The places where European and American explorers visited from the eighteenth through the twentieth centuries are also, for the most part, unchanged. I remember reading Danish explorer Peter Freuchen's account of his and

Knud Rasmussen's harrowing journey to the northernmost section of Green-land. They came upon a cairn—a pile of stones—with a note left behind by Robert Peary's party in the 1890s, years before Peary's final attempt to reach the North Pole. Though Freuchen was there a quarter of a century after Peary, it looked as if Peary had been there the day before. Freuchen could still see the footprints of Peary and his men and the matches they'd dropped on the ground as they paced around, smoking pipes and trying to stay warm. Stunned, Freuchen sat there alone for hours. For him, it must have been the same thing that revisiting the site of the first moon landing would be for us. And actually, at that time, this part of Greenland was almost as remote and inaccessible as the moon. And I'll bet Peary's (and Freuchen's) footprints are still there.

Posted: Friday, July 14, 2000, 10:30 A.M. Pacific time. What do you do when you're cruising through an iceberg-choked fjord in Greenland, wearing every piece of clothing you brought along, and you're still freezing? If you know the answer, please tell me. We just finished searching more than a hundred miles of high, rugged cliffs for nesting falcons and other birds, and I'm still shivering.

But it was great . . . the steep cliffs along both sides of the fjord rising up around us like an Ice Age Grand Canyon . . . the massive icebergs, some the size of small islands, looming up through the mist. There's nothing like it. If only I could keep my teeth from chattering.

I finally connected with the Peregrine Fund research team on Thursday morning—a team consisting of Cornell professor emeritus Tom Cade, who founded the "P-Fund"; the group's president, Bill Burnham, and his son Kurt; and Jack Stephens, a weather forecaster at Thule Air Base. In many ways exploring this area near Uummannaq is the most important part of the entire research expedition. We're trying to retrace the steps of Alfred Bertelsen—a Danish medical doctor who treated Inuit patients in the villages near here in the early twentieth century. He also studied birds avidly and mapped out more than two hundred bird sites, ranging from falcon nests to giant seabird colonies. Our task—using his maps and data published in the 1920s—is to find every site and see how they have fared over the decades.

So far it doesn't look good. Earlier today we took the boat to an enormous cliff face, which used to have a great seabird colony with half a million pairs of murres, as well as razorbills, kittiwakes, and others. We couldn't find any of these species there. We saw only orange lichens growing where the birds' guano had stained the rocks. What happened to the birds? Could Inuit hunters from nearby villages have exterminated the entire colony? It's hard to say exactly what happened at this point.

Some of the falcon nest sites also seemed to be vacant, though we did find some new nests. To locate them, we usually drive the boat to the base of the cliff and fire a rifle. A falcon will generally fly from its nest as the gunshot echoes along the cliff face, have a look around, and then return to its nest. It doesn't seem to cause any more disturbance than the loud crack of a calving glacier—a common sound around here. At one point today a Peregrine Falcon flushed from the cliff as Kurt fired and was joined by her mate, which soared across the sky above us. The high point of the day came later when we saw a pair of snow-white Gyrfalcons perched high atop a massive palisade.

We'll spend a few more days checking the rest of Bertelsen's sites and then embark on the great adventure, taking this boat all the way north to Thule. We'll be cruising across Melville Bay—a place of terror to whalers for centuries because of its icebergs and unpredictable storms. I just heard that the weather is turning nasty up north and may hit us soon. And I made two big mistakes before I left home: I watched *The Perfect Storm*—enough to terrify anyone considering a sea voyage—and I read Rockwell Kent's book *N by E*, about a disastrous trip he and his friends took by sailboat to Greenland in 1929 (the boat ground against a cliff face near here in a storm and sank).

But for now, we're getting a couple of hours' sleep, then starting a sixteen-hour day of searching for birds in a freezing rain in an open boat. Enjoy the weather, wherever you are.

4

RETURN TO
UUMMANNAQ

July 2000

If you had told me in June 2000 that in less than a month I'd be shivering in an open boat, plying my way northward along the coast of Greenland with more than a thousand miles to go to reach Thule, I'd have said . . . well, something insulting. For three summers in a row I had forsaken the warm comforts of my home in upstate New York to huddle with my camera—in the icy winds of subarctic Canada, the barren central highlands of Iceland, the storm-swept northwestern coast of Greenland. I was ready for a change. I was dreaming of visiting someplace warm: a place where ice is unknown except in mixed drinks, where the coolest winds bring only a refreshing respite from the balmy heat, where researchers rise late and stroll to their study areas clad in shorts and straw hats. In short, I wanted to go to the Tropics.

So how did I end up in an open boat, motoring across an ice-choked fjord in northern Greenland, clad in all the high-tech Arctic gear I own, and still freezing? It all started with a tantalizing e-mail I received from Kurt Burnham, manager of The Peregrine Fund's Arctic research program. He mentioned that he would soon be embarking on a little boat trip along the western coast of Greenland, and he had room for one more person. He and three other researchers would be checking a huge study area containing 210 known bird sites—seabird colonies, falcon nests, tern and eider islands—all of which had been documented in meticulous detail in the early twentieth century by Alfred Bertelsen, a Danish physician who spent most of his life in Greenland.

The idea was intriguing. What would it be like to revisit these sites almost a full century after Bertelsen began his work there? What might we learn about the present health of this spectacular Arctic ecosystem at the beginning of the twenty-first century? As an afterthought, Kurt added that this was a once-in-a-lifetime opportunity. That was the clincher.

"I'll be there. See you in Uummannaq," I said, barely realizing what the words meant as I hit the computer key, sending my e-mail reply irretrievably into cyberspace.

From a distance our camp is invisible, hidden in a massive cliff running several miles along the island and rising nearly a thousand feet behind us, disappearing in a dense fog. But get closer and a narrow grassy area takes shape, some seventy-five feet above the water. There we stand, huddled before the cookstove with fresh coffee brewing. Behind us our tents lay nestled in various nooks among the rocks, as sheltered from the elements as possible. We have piled rocks on top of every tent stake—a measure necessary to keep our things from blowing off the cliff the next time a good wind comes screaming through, as we know it will.

With me are Bill and Kurt Burnham; Jack Stephens, a weather forecaster at Thule Air Base (not a bad person to have along on a trip like this); and Cornell professor emeritus Tom Cade, founder of The Peregrine Fund and former research director at the Lab of Ornithology. For Tom this journey has special significance. He had first seen Alfred Bertelsen's Greenland study mentioned in Finn Salomonsen's three-volume *Birds of Greenland*. That was in the early 1950s when Cade was a graduate student. Bertelsen's article—complete with a map of the Uummannaq District with the bird sites marked—had appeared in 1921 in a Danish journal, *Meddelelser om Gronland*. Cade thought it would be interesting to return to Bertelsen's study area someday and see how much the area's bird numbers and species makeup had changed during the intervening years. Now, at age seventy-two and retired, he is fulfilling a half-century-old dream.

By any standard Alfred Bertelsen was a remarkable man. As a young Danish physician in his early twenties, he joined the Greenland Literary Expedition (1902–04)—an ambitious attempt to explore the western coast of Greenland and study the languages and customs of the indigenous people, the Polar Inuit.

The expedition members, led by famed explorer Ludwig Mylius-Erichsen (who would perish on a subsequent Greenland expedition in 1907), spent nearly two years living with a group of Inuit on the shores of North Star Bay. It's remarkable to think that this was just eighty-four years after British naval captains John Ross and Edward Sabine first visited this area. The Inuit who lived there at that time led a Stone Age existence, cut off from the rest of the world by ice and frigid water. They had no boats of any kind or any knowledge of them and were certain that the two British ships had flown down to them from the moon. They believed they were the only humans on Earth and that the rest of the planet was covered by ice.

Bertelsen soon after settled in Uummannaq, a fishing and hunting settlement a couple of hundred miles from Disko Bay, up a spectacular fjord lined with snowcapped cliffs and peaks. He spent several decades of his life there, traveling to the remote villages of the area, treating Inuit patients. Behind his home—which is still occupied by the current doctor—stands another small house that served as his hospital for many years and is now the local museum. But Bertelsen was more than a physician; he was also a capable ornithologist, and spent decades documenting the bird life of the vast Uummannaq District.

He painstakingly mapped out the locations of every bird site he could find in the hundreds of square miles he regularly covered.

And now we are here in the summer of 2000, carrying a copy of his map as we travel from site to site. At each location, we take a GPS reading and note the presence or absence of birds and the approximate numbers, which we will compare with Bertelsen's original surveys.

We head southwestward to check twenty-six bird sites that Bertelsen recorded along the Qarajaqs Isfjord. Lofty cliffs rise on both sides of us, like a primeval Grand Canyon, dusted with snow and ice where they vanish into low-lying clouds and fog. Occasionally a deafening crack and a rumble echo along the fjord as somewhere in the distance another battleship-sized iceberg breaks free of a glacier and plunges into the frigid water. Everything about this place—its scale, its raw beauty, its solitude—is overwhelming. We barely speak as we motor along in our boat, a tiny, insignificant speck in this enormous landscape.

Reaching the mouth of Qarajags Isfjord, our way is blocked by an impenetrable wall of icebergs. We cruise back and forth looking for an entryway, but it's hopeless. These icebergs have been driven here by the prevailing wind. It's possible that some time in the next week or two, a strong wind will blow in the opposite direction, flushing the icebergs and dispersing them through the larger fjord. But we don't have time to wait it out. Bill says we'll have to return in a few days with a helicopter to complete the survey.

We head back north, checking more accessible sites near Uummannaq. We pass an enormous cliff face that, according to Bertelsen, once held a great colony with more than half a million pairs of Thick-billed Murres, as well as numerous Razorbills and Black-legged Kittiwakes. Now it is empty, except for a few hundred Northern Fulmars we see nearby. But what is particularly troublesome is that this is not the first Bertelsen site to disappoint us—just the most dramatic. Many of the sites checked earlier on this survey have had significantly fewer birds present and much less species diversity than Bertelsen reported.

This seems to be particularly true of the sites near human settlements. A lot of the small islands that once held tern colonies and numerous nesting eiders and other waterfowl are now overrun with hungry dogs during the bird breeding season; no chicks or eggs can possibly survive on them. These dogs, which are used by the Inuit to pull heavy wooden sledges during winter, are useless once the ice and snow melt. Dozens of them are turned loose on these islands to fend for themselves each summer.

Though this might explain why so few ground-nesting birds can be found near settlements, why do cliff-nesting species also seem to be vanishing? Did something happen to the small fish population on which they depend for food? Has this area become polluted or contaminated in some way? Or could hunters from nearby villages somehow have exterminated an entire half-million-pair colony? It's a mind-boggling thought.

Some of Bertelsen's falcon nest sites also appear to be vacant, though we do find some new Gyrfalcon and peregrine nests as we explore the cliff-lined fjords. By the time we head back to camp at 10 P.M. we have visited twenty-four of Bertelsen's sites. Not a bad day's work.

We awake to the howl of gale-force winds, rushing through the fjord, driving rain and sleet fiercely down upon us. But offshore we hear another, stranger sound—a great *whoosh*, repeated every few minutes. A massive fin whale, more than sixty feet long, is making its way slowly through the churning icebergs in the fjord, passing within a couple of hundred yards of camp, completely unfazed by the weather.

According to Jack Stephens—who has been batting a thousand on his weather predictions so far—the storm will last all day and probably all night as well. Each day he sets up a mini weather station—a satellite telephone connected to a computer—and downloads the latest images of emerging weather patterns. It's amazing. He's basically using the same radar and satellite data he would use in his office at Thule Air Base.

Obviously, the day is shot for checking nest sites. Bill decides that we should take the boat across to Uummannaq, which is not far away but should be an interesting trip in this storm. There, we can look around the settlement and make arrangements to hire a helicopter for the next day.

After battening down the camp as best we can, we slither down the cliff and climb into the boat. We have to jockey around with icebergs in our tiny cove, pushing them with boat hooks and even driving one out with the bow of the boat before we can get into the open fjord. Wind-driven waves and chop as well as icy rain hammer us all the way across, and there's nowhere to hide in this boat.

The wind and rain have stopped, but it is still cloudy and overcast with the threat of more bad weather. Still, according to Jack, we should have no problem making our helicopter survey this afternoon. It is 2 P.M. as we climb aboard the chopper. Kurt talks his way into the front seat beside the pilot, where the mechanic usually sits. He holds Bertelsen's map in front of him and will point the way for the pilot and take GPS readings at each site. I'm happy to sit in the back on the left side. I've never been one to jump deliberately into the front seat of a roller coaster.

Even wearing the ear protectors the mechanic handed us, the noise is beyond deafening when the motor fires up. Then we're off, over the edge of the cliff and skimming across the fjord, like a fulmar with a rocket engine strapped to its back. And then we're rising—to clifftop level and beyond, taking minutes to pass over an area that had taken us hours to cross in the boat.

Qarajaqs Isfjord, where we had turned back a few days earlier, is still wall-to-wall icebergs, but now we skim easily over it, the shadow of the helicopter standing out sharply in black against the blue-white glacial ice. We fly up to the first Bertelsen site, where Iceland Gulls wheel back and forth against a rugged cliff face. The pilot, a young Norwegian named Tore, hangs the chopper in front of the cliff as Kurt takes a GPS reading and Tom and Bill note the number of birds present. I snap away with my camera at the cliff, at my friends on board, and at the icebergs below. Then Tore turns hard left, flying the chopper sideways and plunging downward as he moves away from the cliff and roars to the next site. (He's a good cab driver, and he knows the meter is running.) As we pass over a small island, several ptarmigans flush below us, their white primaries flashing against the dark rocks and vegetation.

Later I see a Gyrfalcon flush from somewhere far beneath me and fly swiftly across the ice. I shout to everyone to look, but it's impossible to hear anything in there. A couple of hours later we're flying back up the main fjord toward Uummannaq. In less than three hours we've checked twenty-six of Bertelsen's sites and found a few new sites that either didn't exist in his time or perhaps would have been difficult to find without a helicopter.

Back at Uummannaq we eat dinner, and Jack checks the weather situation. He predicts that a major windstorm will strike at about six o'clock the next morning. Bill decides the best course of action is to work an all-nighter, heading north to check several out-of-the-way bird sites. Luckily (or maybe unluckily) it stays light twenty-four hours a day in the Arctic, so nighttime is not a hindrance to determined researchers.

Later that evening, on the way north, two fishing boats accompanied by a smaller skiff emerge from another fjord. The skiff races ahead of the other boats. Suddenly a massive fin whale rises before them, blowing spray from its blowhole, and is met with a fusillade of rifle bullets from all three boats. The whale dives, but the Inuit hunters keep up the chase, not allowing the huge animal to relax for a second. The larger fishing boats move steadily forward, seemingly herding the whale, while the tiny skiff races effortlessly across the water, trying to be there at close range whenever the whale surfaces. It's hard to say how many rounds they fire into the whale or, indeed, how many hits with a rifle it would take to disable such an enormous animal. No harpoons or other specialized whaling gear is visible on any of the boats. Exactly how they intend to land it is anybody's guess. But this scene repeats itself again and again—the whale rising, being hammered by more bullets, and diving—until the Inuit hunters and their prey vanish in the distance into the bleak Arctic twilight.

The next day in Uummannaq we talk with a young Inuit woman who works at the small hotel restaurant where we go to eat dinner and escape from the storm—which blew in a few minutes before 6 A.M., just as Jack had predicted. We tell her about the whale and ask if she knows how the men could possibly get something like that home if they killed it. She says they would probably attach a rope or chain to it and tow it their village. "But sometimes the whales sink to the bottom and wash up three months later, no good for anything," she tells us. "It's very sad."

The storm is still blowing, with no letup in sight, so we're grounded for now. Outside the small harbor loom mountainous icebergs that weren't here yesterday. Although the local people have stretched a rope barrier across the harbor, many smaller icebergs have pushed in and are crowding against boats. Earlier we had one iceberg ride up on our anchor rope, threatening to pull the boat under or capsize it, so we had to move it to a better spot in the anchorage.

Tom and I take the opportunity to visit the small museum in the village and learn more about Bertelsen. The curator, Lucia Ludvigsen, is helpful. She's an Inuit and a native of Uummannaq but was educated in Copenhagen. She speaks perfect English—with a Danish accent—and tells us about the history of the area. We mention the empty bird colonies. The birds were still there in the 1960s, she tells us, and she puts the blame for their disappearance squarely on the ships that often brought tourists from Disko Bay on sight-seeing cruises up the fjords. "When they got to the bird cliffs, the ships would blow their horns to flush the birds so the passengers could see them," she explains. She speculates that the birds' eggs fell out of their nests as the birds flushed and were smashed on the rocks below. "The birds finally abandoned the cliffs," she says.

But then she goes on to tell us that when she was a girl, she and her family would often visit the nearby islands in summer and harvest bird eggs. "Now all the 'well-tasting' birds are gone," she says. "Only the 'storm-birds' [Northern Fulmars] are left."

It seems a telling comment that the only species remaining here is the fulmar—foul tasting and unpleasant to catch, because it spits a noxious oil at predators when it is attacked.

We head out early today, full of high hopes. The weather has improved markedly, and we hope to knock off the final nine Bertelsen sites in one long day, covering some two hundred miles of fjords. The scenery seems to get better and better the farther we go. Looking up at the jagged, snowcapped peaks, rising four thousand feet above the fjord, all I can think of is Valhalla— the sacred place of ancient Norse legend. And the farther we get from Uummannaq, the more wildlife we're seeing. We stop on an island and find newly hatched eiders and some fledgling Glaucous Gulls. A second, larger island has ravens, Lapland Longspurs, and Rock Ptarmigans. We find several active gull colonies, some of which have nesting Black-legged Kittiwakes, a species that was scarce or absent on all of the earlier cliffs we checked.

Then it happens. A slight uneasiness in one of the engines, more felt than heard at first, like a slight stutter. Gradually it gets worse, the engine now misfiring audibly as we push forward at our unrelenting pace. Bertelsen sites fall one after another before us, but the engine cannot be ignored. We change the spark plugs, which seems to help for a few hours, but the misfiring comes back, worse than ever. We finally turn back toward Uummannaq in the afternoon, just three sites short of completing the survey. Soon we're running on only one engine, which cuts our speed well below half, because we don't have enough power to get the hull to plane on top of the water. We're now traveling at less than five miles per hour. It takes us all night and then some to reach Uummannaq.

Though we try for several days to get back on track—calling an ace boat-engine mechanic in Seattle repeatedly via the satellite telephone and getting step-by-step instructions on how to fix the problem; trying everything we can possibly do to make the boat shipshape; and then heading doggedly north-ward, hoping to reach Thule before a major storm is due to hit. But it's hope-less. The motor has water mixed with its crankcase oil. It has a blown head gasket at best, or perhaps a cracked block. Turning southward, we make the long haul back to Uummannaq one more time. We're all in a somber mood this last night on the boat, even though the full moon hanging above the fjord—surrounded by snowcapped peaks in the purplish light of the Arctic—is one of the most exquisite sights I've ever seen.

Soon we will all go our separate ways. Tom Cade has already left on a com-mercial flight back home. But everyone must fly all the way south to Kanger-lussuaq—where the boat trip began—before flying back north to Thule. That's the way things work in Greenland. As for me, though, I manage to hitch a ride on a C-130 military transport plane from Kangerlussuaq directly to upstate New York, instead of having to go to Thule and catch a once-a-week flight to Baltimore on a scary old DC-8 cargo plane and then take a commercial plane to Ithaca.

We still have three of Bertelsen's sites left to check, but Bill and Kurt will return to them in late summer to take GPS readings and see if any nesting took place.

As for what all of the data we gathered this season mean, it is far too early to say. It will take much more research before anyone can say with certainty just what factor or series of factors is to blame for the disappearance of so many nesting birds, but clearly this spectacular place is not as pristine as it ap-pears. Was it the cruise ships? Global warming? Maybe. But a strong circum-stantial case exists that the birds have been overharvested by the indigenous people—to the point that many of their breeding colonies are no longer sus-tainable.

The Inuit are an amazing people, with a tenacious hold on life that has en-abled them to thrive, against all odds, in one of the harshest environments on the planet. To survive, they had to kill as much food as possible, gorging themselves and caching whatever was left to get through the times of starva-

tion. The tenuousness of their existence made this necessary, and it also became part of their being and their overriding ethic to be great hunters. But
now that they have motorboats, rifles, and shotguns, perhaps they have too
much of an advantage over the animals they hunt. If this turns out to be the
case, then the Inuit will have to curtail some of their hunting—otherwise
their unique way of life could vanish along with the seabirds, whales, polar
bears, walruses, and seals they traditionally pursue. All we can do for now is to
watch, gather data, report on our observations, and hope that it will make a
difference.

5

THE PEREGRINES
OF PADRE ISLAND

October 1991

As I drive across the causeway leading from Port Isabel to South Padre Island, Texas, I'm amazed at the number of buildings I see: luxury high-rise hotels, restaurants, souvenir shops, condominiums, real estate offices. A gaudy billboard stuck in the middle of a mudflat announces the island's name and cautions us not to litter, while a bronze statue of Spanish missionary Padre Balli—the "father" of Padre Island—stands with a hand raised to bless passersby as they reach the end of the causeway.

I can't help remembering how different the island looked the last time I was here, some twenty years earlier. The Queen Isabella Causeway had not yet been built, stores and restaurants were hard to find, and there were no high-rise hotels—just a few tiny beach motels on the southernmost stretch of this long, narrow barrier island. But one thing has not changed in the two decades since I last visited Padre Island, and it is the same thing that drew me here both times. This thin strip of storm-swept sand dunes is the scene of a great natural spectacle: the autumn gathering of migrating Arctic Peregrine Falcons en route from their far northern nesting areas to their wintering grounds in Latin America.

Padre Island is a typical barrier island—long, narrow, and dune covered. Starting just offshore from Corpus Christi, it follows the Texas coast almost all the way to Mexico, more than 120 miles south. But three-quarters of the way down the island's length Mansfield Channel slices through, allowing shrimp boats, pleasure craft, and other shipping to enter and leave Laguna Madre from the Gulf of Mexico. Called "the cut" by locals, the channel divides Padre into a north and a south island. The bulk of the north island has been preserved as the Padre Island National Seashore, while South Padre Island is a popular Texas tourist trap. Sun seekers and other visitors flock here by the thousands to enjoy the warm weather, the picturesque beaches, or the fishing. A few come for the birds.

In this respect South Padre Island is no disappointment, especially for peregrine-watchers. The island is a convenient migration midpoint for the falcons, where they can rest and build up fat stores before continuing on a journey that may stretch from above the Arctic Circle all the way south to Argentina or Chile. The falcons, which are mostly the tundra subspecies of peregrine, live for the bulk of the year in South America, spending only the mild summer months on their breeding grounds in Alaska, Canada, or Greenland.

Though large numbers of peregrines pass through other places in North America on migration—Assateague Island, Cape May—Padre Island is unique in two respects: First, unlike the other areas, many falcons stay on Padre for weeks at a time, using it as a staging area; and second, peregrines gather here in significant numbers during both autumn and spring migrations. The other peregrine migration hot spots in North America are outstanding in autumn, when hordes of newly fledged juveniles make their first trek southward, but during the northward migration in spring see barely a trickle of falcons. Consequently, Padre Island has been a boon for falcon research.

◆ ◆ ◆

Before I arrive at the beach house where I'll be meeting a group of falcon researchers, I spot a beautiful adult female peregrine perched on the rigging under a water tower. She is amazingly approachable. I set up my camera and tripod right under her and snap pictures at will. Her lack of suspicion is fairly typical of Arctic birds, which have little contact with humans most of the year. As I pack up my gear and leave, she is still perched there, calmly watching me.

Tom Maechtle, head of the Padre Island Peregrine Falcon Survey (PIPFS), has been studying the falcons on the island since 1985. Each spring and fall he brings a team of researchers to Padre, where they spend an entire month studying peregrines, watching their behavior, trapping and banding them, and collecting falcon blood samples for DNA and contaminant analysis.

"I've been fortunate to have such a dedicated group of people working with me on Padre Island," says Maechtle. "The same people return year after year, and each one is an expert falcon trapper. Some of them take vacation time from their regular jobs to come down here. Our success depends on them."

Fortunately, the Peregrine Falcon has had little trouble over the years attracting the attention of humans who are dedicated to its well-being. When DDT and other persistent chemicals in the environment caused the Peregrine Falcon population to crash in the 1960s, prominent ornithologists such as Tom Cade of Cornell University rushed to turn around the species' perilous decline. Cade established The Peregrine Fund and enlisted the aid of scores of falcon enthusiasts willing to work long hours for minimal wages to help bring the falcons back. Thanks to their efforts, Peregrine Falcons once again breed in the eastern United States (where they had been extirpated), and their numbers are up throughout North America.

Tom Maechtle, who now lives in Boise, Idaho, worked for The Peregrine Fund for several years when it was headquartered at the Cornell Laboratory of Ornithology. He stayed at the Hawk Barn in Sapsucker Woods, where peregrines were being bred in captivity to provide young falcons for the reintroduction program. "I tended peregrine hack [release] sites every summer while I was in high school," says Maechtle. "I stayed at the first hack site at Taughannock Falls near Ithaca in the mid-1970s. Then, after I graduated, I came to work at The Peregrine Fund full time."

Many of the falcon researchers I spoke with had similar stories to tell. Most had been obsessed with falcons since childhood. For Oscar Beingolea, who came all the way from Peru to trap falcons on Padre Island, the Peregrine Falcon is the supreme winged predator—a bird of power, grace, and beauty. Like the other team members, he is fascinated by the mystery of where the peregrines come from and where they go on migration. He believes that the only way we can even begin to understand the peregrine migration is to retrap large numbers of banded falcons in South America.

"We have retrapped several birds in Peru that were banded in North America," says Beingolea. "Three from Padre Island, Texas; two from Cape May, New Jersey; and one from Rankin Inlet [Hudson Bay], Canada, in 1982, which I trapped in Peru in March 1989. This bird was resighted at his nest in Canada later that summer. So we now know where he nests and perhaps where he winters each year. We need to track more falcons that closely."

The Padre Island survey is only a small part of team member Bud Anderson's work with falcons. He is also director of the Falcon Research Group, a nonprofit organization based in Bow, Washington. He spends most winters in South America tracking Arctic peregrines on their wintering grounds. "There's a loose network of falcon researchers," says Anderson. "We study peregrines in Alaska, Canada, Greenland, South America, and the migration spots in between. We all know each other and keep track of each other's work. Tom Maechtle hires me in spring and fall to band peregrines on Padre Island, and that dovetails nicely with my research in South America."

What is perhaps most remarkable about Maechtle, Anderson, and many of the others is that they are not affiliated with a university or major research institution. They must seek government and private funding independently to carry on their work.

Each morning as dawn breaks over Padre Island, the trappers have already loaded up their all-terrain vehicles (ATVs) and are headed up the beach toward the prime falcon areas. Survey team members often spend more than twelve hours a day driving slowly up and down the island, stopping frequently to scan for falcons. It is a harsh environment, where the trappers may face searing heat, blowing sand, mosquitoes, rain, and a chill Gulf wind, all in the same day. Still, it's an experience that few survey team members can stand to pass up come spring and autumn.

As I drive my ATV across the broad expanse of tidal flats on the backside of Padre Island, I can't help thinking of a scene from the movie Lawrence of Arabia. *Lawrence and the Bedouins, riding atop huge camels, are trudging across a barren, trackless landscape called "the anvil of the sun," pounded mercilessly by endless shimmering heat. Now I know how they felt. The vast area behind the dunes on Padre Island seems almost as remote (and hot) as the Arabian desert. Hard to imagine that only twenty miles south on the developed end of the island, high-rise hotels and condominiums tower above the shifting sands.*

Though peregrines are seen just about everywhere on Padre Island—flying along the shore, perched on tall buildings, or sitting on sand dunes—the PIPFS trappers prefer to patrol the huge tidal flats on the landward side of the island, where most of the peregrines gather. An ATV is the only practical vehicle to drive on the flats. Anything else would get stuck immediately in the soft, damp sand. Each ATV is a self-contained mobile trapping station, with portable traps, optical gear, bands, blood sampling equipment, a two-way radio, food, and water—everything you need for a full day of trapping.

I sit on my ATV scanning the horizon with binoculars. The flats look as lonesome as the moon. A brown object moving at the edge of the dune line catches my eye—a coyote searching for refuse washed ashore. At high tide, water rushes onto these flats, erasing our tire tracks and bringing new objects for coyotes and other beachcombers to scavenge. Looking back toward Laguna Madre, I see a nondescript shape on the sand near the water's edge. I can't make out any detail, but something about the tilt of it, the way it seems to be leaning into the wind, convinces me it is a peregrine. I turn and drive quickly upwind for a better look.

When most people think of a hunting Peregrine Falcon, they picture the bird hurtling down on its prey from a lofty altitude. The hunting style of the birds on the flats of Padre Island is about as far removed from that image as you can get. Here the falcons usually sit on the sand or on any available perch—a post, an old crate, a piece of driftwood—and wait. When potential prey flies over, the falcon takes off from ground level and attempts to intercept it. This is an unusual hunting tactic. Peregrines normally rely on surprise and an altitude advantage to overtake their prey, dropping from a high perch or diving down out of a soar. In most situations a high-flying bird would be long gone before a falcon sitting at ground level could build up enough speed to overtake it. But on the broad tidal flats of Padre Island, the predator–prey relationship shifts to the falcons' advantage.

These flats have served the peregrines for millennia as a vast, open bird trap. Songbirds, shorebirds, waterfowl, and other migrants making the crossing to Padre Island are already exhausted from their long journeys. But before reaching the safety of the dune grass and other vegetation in the middle of the island, they must first cross Laguna Madre and then pass over a wide "no-man's-land" of flat, barren sand. It is a dangerous crossing for any bird that attempts to run this gauntlet. At times several falcons will fly out to intercept one bird.

Sometimes the prey is another raptor. On this trip I saw a peregrine dive repeatedly at a tiny Sharp-shinned Hawk. The smaller bird managed to sidestep the falcon's stoops time after time, and it finally reached cover. But Mark

Robertson, a longtime PIPFS trapper, recalls seeing a Merlin that wasn't so lucky. Half a dozen peregrines chased the smaller falcon back and forth, high over the flats, until it was finally caught.

It is a grim but efficient process. Migrating peregrines must conserve energy and build up fat stores before continuing their own perilous journeys, where they too might face death through starvation, collisions with power lines and vehicles, attacks by other predators, or poisoning by toxic chemicals.

We spot a hatch-year male peregrine perched on a low piece of driftwood at the edge of an inlet and set out a portable trap for him. Before we can even drive away, this falcon and two others start diving at the trap. We set another trap and all three birds work them as we watch. Two birds are down on the traps, then the male tries to fly and is caught. We move in quickly.

The PIPFS team always splits into two groups during peregrine migrations; one stays in a beach rental on South Padre, while the other sets up camp on North Padre Island. The camp is rough—sandy, windblown, and full of mosquitoes at night. Ferrying the ATVs, tents, and other equipment across the channel is always an adventure. To get to North Padre Island each trapper drives his ATV onto a large plywood board on top of a Zodiac rubber boat, then floats it carefully across the channel. The crossing can be a hair-raising experience, especially if a powerboat cruises down the channel and kicks up a wake. But so far none of the ATVs (or falcon trappers) has ended up at the bottom of the channel.

The survey crews have developed their falcon-trapping techniques to a fine art. They know how to recognize peregrines at extreme distances, how to set up traps quickly, and how to lure in a falcon effectively. But the after-capture work is even more impressive as the trapper hurries to process the falcon, record data, and release the bird in fifteen minutes or less to avoid undue stress. The first step is to slip a leather falconry hood over the peregrine's head (the darkness provided by a hood has a remarkable calming effect on a falcon).

Then the bird is taken from the trap and placed in a light cotton straitjacket to hold it steady. Next the trapper bands the falcon, takes a tiny blood sample, and daubs the bird's breast with a harmless dye. The color mark helps trappers distinguish an already caught falcon from a fresh one to save wasted effort. The dye generally fades away in three or four weeks in the sunlight, rain, and salt spray the birds are exposed to. The falcon is then set free. It is a remarkably smooth, efficient procedure.

We catch a hatch-year male peregrine at midday. Processing the bird is hell. The day has turned hot and sticky. As we hurry to band the falcon and take a blood sample, the air around us fills with tiny buzzing gnats. They cover our faces, crawling into our eyes and up our noses and ears. The sound is deafening. It is impossible to breathe without inhaling them. Our eyes fill with sweat. Finally we finish up, release the bird, and blast down the beach on our ATVs at full speed to blow away the gnats.

Collecting falcon blood samples is an important part of the PIPFS team's work. Researchers hope eventually to be able to pinpoint the areas where particular falcons were born by analyzing their DNA. Then if an unbanded peregrine is captured in South America during winter, a simple blood test could reveal whether the bird is a native of the area or a migrant from Alaska, Canada, or Greenland.

"We also record the levels of toxins that accumulate in the blood of individual falcons," says Maechtle. "We'll look at those samples where we have a falcon, for example, that was caught in 1985 as a hatch-year bird, then caught again in 1987 and 1990, and we'll measure whether the bird's contamination level has increased over time. We get enough retraps on the same birds to make that possible. We may not get them every year, but we often recapture them every third or fourth year."

We're in the doldrums now. Everyone is hoping for a storm front from the north. The birds ride the storms all the way down from Alaska and northern Canada. The trappers depend on them for a good migration. A strong storm front will flush out the birds that are already here, sending them on their way to South America, and bring in a new batch of unbanded falcons. Many of the ones we see on the flats now are already color marked.

The falcon retrap rate on Padre Island is astounding. In spring fully 30 percent of the falcons caught were previously banded on the island, which shows how faithful the birds are to a migration route. "It's not just by chance that we're capturing them here," says Maechtle. "The falcons have as great a level of fidelity to a staging area as they do to their nesting grounds."

Maechtle believes that this may also be true of the falcons' wintering grounds. Perhaps the birds are on their way to their own particular favorite perching areas in South America. That's why the work of Maechtle and the others is important—so that prime pieces of falcon wintering areas, as well as staging areas, can be identified and ultimately preserved.

"If we don't continue to monitor Peregrine Falcons, we could easily slip back into the same scenario we faced in the 1960s, when the birds' population crashed," says Maechtle. "Only by keeping track of the birds' numbers and by continually analyzing the levels of toxins in their blood can we avoid that."

While I'm standing in front of the hotel waiting for the shuttle bus that will take me to Harlingen Airport, a female Peregrine Falcon comes ripping over the top of a nearby high-rise hotel. She turns over and makes a vertical dive into the small field of dune grass between the two buildings. Through my binoculars, I can see her swoop repeatedly at a small bird. Each time the bird sidesteps her attack, the falcon pulls out of the dive and lets her momentum carry her almost back to her former altitude. Finally the small bird gets safely into some shrubbery that surrounds the hotel. The falcon barely misses slamming into the side of the building as she pulls up. She lands on the hotel roof and starts preening her flight feathers. Suddenly I'm aware of a van parked next to me with its driver honking the horn. I take a final look at the falcon, still perched on the high-rise, as we drive away to the airport.

6
BIRDING AT THE EDGE OF THE ARCTIC

June 1997

Churchill, Manitoba, has a lot of character. How many other places can you think of that have an official civil defense system set up to warn people about polar bears—which sometimes come ambling through town in late summer or fall? But if you're looking for something charming or quaint—a Cape May of the North—forget it. Perched at the western edge of Hudson Bay, Churchill is a drab, dusty, treeless frontier outpost alongside a vast wilderness of tundra, boreal forest, muskeg bogs, and lakes stretching for thousands of miles across the north of the continent. A narrow strip of asphalt lined with a few shops, motels, and a gas station makes up the main road. Local residents of all ages ride all-terrain vehicles up and down the wide expanse of dirt beside the road, kicking up clouds of dust as they go. But Churchill has great charm for people with an eye for the muted beauty of the tundra—especially those who appreciate seeing Arctic wildlife up close.

Though Churchill is a considerable distance south of the Arctic Circle, the frigid winds that blow across ice-covered Hudson Bay have created a tundra habitat much like that found far to the north. But go a short distance inland and you enter a transition zone where tundra meets boreal forest, creating a rich mixture of plants and animals. This is a harsh land, with an extremely short "warm" season that draws migratory birds from as far away as South America to take advantage of the mosquitoes and other foods available in abundance.

Few places are better than the Churchill area for observing nesting shore-birds in the full splendor of their breeding plumages. Here the usually drab gray Short-billed Dowitchers assume the stunning cinnamon colors of their nuptial garb, Dunlins sport black bellies, and American Golden-Plovers . . . well, to my mind no shorebird has a more beautiful breeding plumage.

Many migrants arrive at or pass through the Churchill area in May; June through early July, however, is probably the best time for birders to visit. During that brief window you can find all the nesting shorebirds mentioned above along with Whimbrels, Hudsonian Godwits, Stilt Sandpipers, Pacific Loons, Bonaparte's Gulls, Smith's Longspurs, and more. You may even see a rare Ross's Gull—a Churchill specialty.

For the birds nesting near Churchill, the breeding season is brief and in-tense. The birds arrive en masse. They mate, lay eggs, and raise young—and then they depart. By mid-July most male shorebirds have already left.

I spent the last ten days of June in Churchill this past summer, and it was an excellent time to be there. The change of seasons is amazingly compressed. When I arrived the weather was uncomfortably cold, and the Churchill River was still choked with ice. By the time I left the days were pleasant (for the most part), wildflowers were blooming profusely, and the river was ice-free, with large pods of beluga whales swimming slowly upstream past the docks.

♦ ♦ ♦

From a bird photographer's standpoint, Churchill is outstanding. Within easy walking distance of the town center—right behind the huge granary—lies a series of ponds excellent for bird photography. During a recent stay at Churchill I took pictures at these ponds almost every day, usually in late afternoon and early evening. As I sat without a blind at the water's edge, Stilt Sandpipers, Lesser Yellowlegs, Short-billed Dowitchers, and Hudsonian Godwits strode boldly past, within easy full-frame range of my 500mm lens. Tiny Red-necked Phalaropes spun in the shallows, stirring up food; Arctic Terns landed on rocks and driftwood nearby, interacting noisily with others of their kind; and various ducks—Greater Scaups, Northern Shovelers, Gadwalls, American Wigeons, Northern Pintails, and more—swam past or stood preening only yards away. (These ponds are also one of the best places to catch a glimpse of or photograph a Ross's Gull.)

I think if I'd spent my entire trip photographing only at the granary ponds, I'd still have come back with an impressive number of bird images. I chose instead to explore the area more fully, driving up Goose Creek Road and Hydro Road as far as the pump station, around Cape Merry, along the coast of Hudson Bay to Bird Cove, and inland to Twin Lakes—an area of taiga (boreal forest) covered with stunted spruce. I had hoped to photograph a pair of Three-toed Woodpeckers that were nesting near Twin Lakes, but a forest fire—which I'd seen from the airplane as I flew to Churchill—destroyed the nest area. Flames flew high into the sky and trees exploded as the fire raged. Apparently ignited by a spark from a chain saw, the fire devastated a huge area of forest. But a few days later, as I visited the site, I saw Gray Jays foraging in the scorched forest. Fortunately, the forest fire should ultimately prove beneficial for the local Three-toed and Black-backed woodpeckers, which thrive in burned areas.

The human history of Churchill and the surrounding area is fascinating. For centuries Hudson Bay has lured people to ply its waters and explore its rugged coast. Native Peoples, the Pre-Dorsets, hunted and fished there some three thousand years ago. Europeans came much later, in the early 1600s, searching for the elusive Northwest Passage. But Hudson Bay was harsh to the early European explorers. Even Henry Hudson, the bay's namesake, fell victim to the place, in 1611. After facing the hardship of a winter with their ship stuck in ice, his crew mutinied. Hudson was set adrift in a small sloop, *Mutiny on the Bounty* style, with his son and several other crewmen who had refused to take part in the mutiny. But unlike Captain Bligh, Hudson and his men did not make a fantastic open-boat journey across thousands of miles of open sea to reach a British outpost as heroes. Instead, they drifted off into the subarctic bleakness, never to be heard from again.

Jens Munk, a seventeenth-century explorer from Denmark and the first European to land at what is now Churchill, fared only marginally better. After a bone-chilling winter camped on the shores of the Churchill River, most of the sixty-five crewmen who had sailed the two ships—the *Unicorn* and the *Lamprey*—to the New World had perished. At his bleakest moment, in April 1620, Munk wrote in his journal:

> Inasmuch as I have now no more hope of life in this world, I request, for the sake of God, if any Christian should happen to come here, that they will bury in the earth my poor body, together with the others which are found here, expecting their reward from God in heaven; and furthermore that this my journal may be forwarded to my most gracious Lord and King . . . in order that my poor wife and children may obtain some benefit from my great distress and miserable death. Herewith, good night to all the world; and my soul into the hand of God.

But warmer weather finally came, and Munk and the other two survivors managed to regain their strength by consuming whatever newly sprouted plants, fish, and birds they could find. (It was at this time that Munk compiled the area's first bird list, noting the return dates for eight migratory species.) On

June 16 the three men began a miraculous journey, sailing through freezing weather, fog, and icebergs in the bay, and then across the Atlantic all the way to Denmark, in a ship that should have had a crew of at least sixteen.

One of the most interesting human-built structures at Churchill is Fort Prince of Wales, a three-hundred-foot-square stone fortress built by the Hudson's Bay Company to guard the mouth of the Churchill River. The fort is on the other side of the river from the town and accessible only by boat, but it's well worth visiting. The unique, low-lying, star-shaped fort was completed in 1771 after forty years of construction. The company also built two other gun emplacements, one farther up the river on the same side as the fort and the other directly across the river from the fort. The fort and the smaller batteries were meant to protect the fur trading empire of the Hudson's Bay Company from competing enterprises, foreign or domestic.

Unfortunately in August 1782, the first and only time the fort came under attack, the defenders were completely outmanned and outgunned. Three French warships—a seventy-four-gunner and two thirty-six-gunners—landed several hundred armed troops near the fort, under cover of darkness. The fort's entire force numbered only thirty-nine men. As the sun rose over the horizon, Samuel Hearne, the fort's commander, took one look at the ships' cannons aimed at the fort and the numerous armed men gathered below and ran up the white flag. I guess he took the advice of Shakespeare's Falstaff to heart: "The better part of valor is discretion."

More recently, in the early 1930s, Churchill became a seaport—the only one in subarctic Canada. There wheat from the southern prairies of Manitoba is brought by train to the port, where ships are loaded to take the grain to Europe. But the shipping season is short—four months at most. Then the bay and the river ice over again, and the port shuts down. Churchill has come to depend more and more on tourism to stay economically viable.

People from all over the world come to Churchill each year to see polar bears, which have become the area's star attraction. Several companies take sightseers out in massive "Tundra Buggies" to look at bears. But though

Churchill has been dubbed the Polar Bear Capital of the World by the local chamber of commerce, it's rare to see a bear during peak birding season. Bears start to appear in late summer as the ice departs from the bay and stay through November, when the ice re-forms. When the bay is frozen the enormous animals spend most of their time on the ice, hunting for seals. It's fine with me that the bear and bird seasons don't coincide. I don't cherish the idea of running into a polar bear when I'm out photographing birds. I also wouldn't like to be in Churchill when it's packed with tourists. During the bird nesting season, the place is pretty quiet.

Churchill is inaccessible by automobile. To get there, you must travel either by airplane or by train—a thirty-eight-hour ride from Winnipeg. This is one of the last great wilderness train rides in North America and is a fascinating journey, if you have the time and endurance to enjoy it. Some people opt to drive to Thompson, Manitoba, and take a train from there, though it's still a long haul to get to Churchill. But you do have a chance of spotting some interesting birds along the way, including Northern Hawk Owls and Great Gray Owls.

If you're visiting Churchill for the first time, consider taking a specialty tour. It's difficult to find the best birding locales yourself, and it's expensive to rent a vehicle there. But if you don't like organized tours, another option is to visit Churchill by yourself (or with friends who will split the cost of a van rental) and follow the directions in Bonnie Chartier's excellent book *A Birder's Guide to Churchill,* published by the American Birding Association. Bonnie has lived in Churchill for years. She knows the area well and shares her wealth of local birding knowledge in the guide, which features numerous maps and tips on where to go and what to look for in the area. She also provides lists of hotels, restaurants, vehicle rental agencies, and more.

If you choose to visit Churchill with an organized tour, be sure to sign up with one tailored to your particular interests, be they birding, photography, or bear-watching. Because the goal of most birding tours is to cover as much ground and see as many species as possible, these tours are not always the best choice if the primary reason for your trip is to take pictures. To photograph birds effectively you sometimes need to spend a lot of time in one area, perhaps working with only one or two species at a time. You won't see as many species, but you'll come home with a good collection of photographs. On the other hand, if adding birds to your life list is the primary goal of your trip, you should definitely sign up with a good birding tour.

Whatever your reason for traveling there, I'm sure you'll have a great time in Churchill. Just be sure to bring plenty of mosquito repellent.

II

RARE
RAPTORS

7

SAVING CALIFORNIA'S PEREGRINE FALCONS

June 1978

The falcon swoops low across the face of the great rock. Far beneath him stretches Morro Bay, still shrouded in morning fog. A lone fishing boat chugs through the harbor, the only break in a dense silence. Rising above the water, the falcon dives repeatedly at a trespassing gull, then, tiring of his sport, returns to his lofty ledge, satisfied that he still rules Morro Rock.

Beside him a lone nestling pleads for food, flapping its wings to attract his attention. The adult peregrine looks away, unconcerned. Now the female appears, carrying a tempting morsel of meat. She lands out of the young falcon's reach, teasing it to come toward her. The nestling screams plaintively and stares down at the chasm between them. Finally, unable to control its appetite any long, the falcon plunges from the precipice into the first flight of its life.

And so another Peregrine Falcon is fledged from this rugged granite crag on the coast of central California. But something is unusual about this young falcon; it was hatched nearly 3,000 miles away in a laboratory at Cornell University in Ithaca, New York.

This spring, for the second year in a row, researchers provided the Morro Rock peregrines with foster nestlings. As a result of DDT contamination, the resident pair of falcons can no longer produce eggshells thick and durable enough to protect a growing embryo. They must now depend on humans to help them raise their young.

In 1969 a female Peregrine Falcon nesting on Morro Rock became a direct victim of this eggshell-thinning syndrome. An egg broke in her oviduct, creating a blockage of waste material in her body that led to a slow death. The male found a new mate after one companionless season, but nesting success on the rock has been sporadic ever since.

The Santa Cruz Predatory Bird Research Group (SCPBRG) is leading the fight to save the Peregrine Falcon in California. Part of the department of environmental studies at the University of California at Santa Cruz (UCSC), the group hopes to follow the lead set by Cornell University, which has a major captive breeding facility and is releasing young Peregrine Falcons at sites across the East. James Rousch, a local veterinarian, submitted plans for the breeding facility in 1973. UCSC officials were enthusiastic and agreed to let him use an abandoned rock quarry on campus as the project's site. They also provided an office and access to a laboratory.

The SCPBRG's original breeding facility consisted of four twenty-foot-long by twenty-foot-wide by twelve-foot-high compartments, with wooden slats overhead to allow the free passage of light and air. The first peregrines placed in the facility were sick or injured falcons collected by the U.S. Fish and Wildlife Service. Although pairs of them were turned loose in the breeding chambers, their physical condition made it unlikely that any of them would produce fertile eggs.

Brian Walton, a twenty-seven-year-old biologist, became coordinator of the SCPBRG last year. With him came an enthusiastic band of volunteers. Since their arrival they have added eight new breeding chambers to the original four, obtained eleven new peregrines, and handed the group its first successes—three captive-bred Prairie Falcons and two Harris's Hawks. Walton believes that they will produce their first young peregrines this coming spring.

The workday begins early at the breeding project. Long before the sun illuminates the picturesque campus and floods into the old rock quarry, the volunteers are busy cleaning the breeding chambers and preparing food for the falcons. The younger peregrines grow visibly excited as Merlyn Felton, the main falcon handler, enters with their daily ration of fresh meat. A young male lets out a harsh, long-winded scream, sounding like a rusty hinge in need of oiling. He seems to consider Felton a long-lost parent. The other falcons maintain a stoical calm as he walks into each of their chambers.

The unflagging dedication of the SCPBRG volunteers is amazing. Felton spends virtually all his time with the birds, actually sleeping in the facility at night to guard against intruders.

Guarding falcons is not a new line of work for Felton—he has spent the past three springs camped atop damp, windswept Morro Rock, watching its falcon nest. "This year I stayed on the rock twenty-four hours a day from April 15 to July 1," he says. "I feel that we owe the wild creatures we've harmed some help. If I didn't have such a special interest in the Peregrine Falcon, I'd probably be involved in saving the wolf or some other threatened animal."

Brian Walton has a similar interest in the well-being of the falcons. "If the peregrine hadn't been endangered, I probably wouldn't have become a biologist," says Walton, laughing. "I would've been a business major and studied falcons as a hobby."

John Schmitt, a bird-watcher and artist, is perhaps the most multifaceted of the volunteers. He helps feed and handle the falcons, shows the facility to the public, and creates artwork to raise money for the project. Schmitt has been fascinated by birds and the beauty of their flight for most of his life. "I was naturally attracted to the Peregrine Falcon because it represents the epitome of flight," he says.

One thing you notice right away when you speak with anyone who's involved in the Peregrine Falcon recovery is the contagious sense of urgency—the feeling that you should drop everything you're doing immediately and run to the falcons' aid. Ron Walker—at twenty-four, the youngest volunteer—did just that. He dropped out of California Polytechnic College two years ago to help with falcon research full time. Last spring, he stayed at one of The Peregrine Fund's release sites on the East Coast, hoping to gain knowledge that can be applied to California's peregrines.

An incredible amount of work stands before Walton and the others. With 90 percent of California's Peregrine Falcon nests abandoned, the situation is critical. Walton hopes to boost the peregrine's population in California from twenty nesting pairs to sixty within ten years. He plans to accomplish this through the rehabilitation of sick and injured falcons, through manipulation of wild populations, and by adopting Cornell University's techniques of breeding falcons in captivity and releasing them to the wild.

Cornell's Peregrine Fund has been an invaluable aid in getting the SCPBRG on its feet. This year the group donated two pairs of specially raised peregrines to the Santa Cruz project, making the prospect for breeding success this coming spring very bright. Cornell also provided Walton with young falcons to put in the Morro Rock nest.

When Walton saw that the eggs didn't hatch at Morro Rock in 1977, he placed some young Prairie Falcons (a nonendangered species that is similar to the peregrine in size) in the nest so that the parents wouldn't lose interest in the site. As is usually the case when researchers employ this "cross-fostering" technique, the falcons accepted the young without any problems. The Peregrine Fund then delivered two young peregrines, still covered with white nestling down, to the rock, and the researchers made another successful switch. They used the same technique again in 1978 to preserve the continuity of the nest site.

In future years, Walton wants to remove the eggs from the Morro Rock nest and several others. Falcons will generally recycle and lay a second clutch of eggs if the first ones are taken early in the season. This could greatly increase egg production. Additionally, the eggs taken have a much better chance of hatching in an incubator. Not only do thin-shelled eggs tend to crack under the weight of a brooding falcon, but they also allow too much moisture to escape, dehydrating and killing the embryo. Some of the thin-shelled eggs Walton cared for this past spring lost weight so rapidly that he had to double the natural humidity in the incubator.

Aside from being used to raise falcons, the SCPBRG facility is an effective educational tool, enabling students and interested members of the public to view the falcons, unseen, through two-way mirrors and providing a unique opportunity to study falcon behavior firsthand. Visitors to the facility learn the reasons why the Peregrine Falcon and other endangered species should be saved—why it's vitally important to maintain the ecological integrity of the planet.

Peregrine Falcons are a necessary controller of small birds, weeding out weaker and sicklier individuals and maintaining healthy populations. If not checked by falcons, overgrown bird flocks could destroy vital habitats and spread disease to wildlife as well as humans. Moreover, humans—like Peregrine Falcons—exist at the top of the food chain. Thus these birds can warn us of dangerous conditions ahead for ourselves.

Many more reasons exist for saving the Peregrine Falcon—things that cannot be explained in practical terms. The power and grace of its flight has enthralled humans for centuries. We owe it to our children not to let the peregrine become a casualty in our rush to progress and be lost forever.

8

MISSION
ACCOMPLISHED

June 1999

T he future could not have looked much bleaker for the American Peregrine Falcon in 1970. Ravaged by the effects of DDT and other environmental contaminants, falcon numbers had dwindled to the point that no nesting pairs had been found in the entire eastern United States for more than a decade. Lofty cliffs that had echoed with the cries of nesting peregrines for thousands of years before humans ever reached these shores stood quiet—like silent sentinels to the birds' impending extinction. Even in places where civilization had not yet visibly encroached on their habitat, in the remotest reaches of the Rocky Mountains, the birds were vanishing, and many biologists feared the trend was irreversible.

Looking back now, it's clear that 1970 was a crucial turning point for the Peregrine Falcon—the year that Cornell professor Tom Cade initiated an aggressive, hands-on program to breed these critically endangered birds in captivity and reintroduce them across the continent in areas where they were dwindling or already nonexistent. It was in 1970 that Cade, director of research at the Cornell Lab of Ornithology, formed The Peregrine Fund, dedicated to saving these rapidly vanishing birds. The group built a massive "Hawk Barn" at the edge of Sapsucker Woods Sanctuary to house the captive breeding project. Although the building remains, it no longer houses breeding falcons. The Cornell Raptor Program now uses the facility to breed accipiters—Goshawks, Cooper's Hawks, and Sharp-shinned Hawks—as well as to house injured eagles and other birds of prey in need of rehabilitation.

In its heyday the Hawk Barn was a virtual Peregrine Falcon factory, where hundreds of young falcons were produced to be released into the wild. What Cade and his army of falcon enthusiasts accomplished was incredible. They figured out how to breed large numbers of falcons in captivity, designed an effective reintroduction strategy, and eventually released more than five thousand Peregrine Falcons in thirty-seven states and most Canadian provinces.

Perhaps the one factor that made the greatest difference in the Peregrine Falcon recovery was the large number of people dedicated to the birds' wellbeing. From the start Cade had no problem attracting qualified staff and volunteers. Many—including some of the key players in the recovery program such as Cade himself, Bill Burnham (current president of The Peregrine Fund), and Jim Weaver (who ran the falcon breeding operation at Cornell)—were avid falconers with a deep personal commitment to the peregrine. Many falconers also donated their own birds to be used as breeders. People from all walks of life and all income levels—bird-watchers, business leaders, scientists, educators, public officials, naturalists, students—came together to support this effort. What they had in common was a profound passion for these birds and an inability to imagine a world without the Peregrine Falcon. What they accomplished was one of the greatest successes in the field of endangered-species management.

Now, nearly three decades after the Peregrine Falcon recovery effort was launched, their accomplishment seems simple, almost predictable—produce thousands of falcons and release them across the country; the birds are bound to bounce back. But it's always easy to be a Monday-morning quarterback. In 1970 the whole enterprise was anything but sure. Although Peregrine Falcons had been trained and handled by falconers for centuries, they had never been truly domesticated. They always retained their aloofness—that air of nobility that ancient kings and aristocrats had so admired. And these birds had been bred in captivity only a handful of times before, most notably by Heinz Meng, who had been a student of Lab of Ornithology founder Arthur Allen in the late 1940s and early 1950s.

Were these successful breedings a fluke? Many researchers thought so. They believed it would never be possible to breed massive numbers of peregrines in captivity. And even if you could, they reasoned, it would be impossible to release them successfully into the wild in numbers large enough to make a difference. The problem was that peregrines had traditionally always nested on lofty, rugged cliffs, performing grand courtship displays, rising and diving at scorching speeds across the open sky. No laboratory breeding facility in the world could duplicate these conditions. Would Peregrine Fund researchers be able to overcome these challenges? And just as important, could they do it in time?

To understand the Peregrine Falcon's dilemma and ultimate solution, you must look back at the origins of the bird's decline—the introduction of DDT into the environment in the late 1940s. The first inklings of trouble for the peregrines came soon after, but it was not until the mid-1960s that scientists learned the full scope of the catastrophe. Researchers discovered that the effects of DDT are cumulative, building up in the fatty tissue of small birds that consume contaminated insects. Peregrine Falcons, which exist at the top of the food chain, preyed on these birds and absorbed staggering amounts of concentrated DDT.

DDT inhibits the movement of calcium in a falcon's system, causing the shell gland to produce eggs with shells sometimes 20 percent thinner than normal. The weight of a falcon as it brooded these fragile eggs was often enough to break the shells. And even if the thin-shelled eggs did not crack, many embryos perished due to an improper moisture or gas exchange through the shell.

Proving that DDT was the culprit took a great deal of time and research. Cade had marked off an area along the Colville River in northern Alaska as a study site in the 1950s. He returned in the mid-1960s and began randomly sampling falcon eggs for pesticide contamination. The Arctic peregrines were well isolated from humans on their breeding grounds, and yet their eggs contained high levels of DDT, which they had no doubt ingested during their long migrations to South America and back. Cade compared the pesticide levels in these eggs with the pesticide levels in thin-shelled eggs from the lower forty-eight states and made a startling prediction: The northern peregrine nests would soon start failing. This grim prophecy was realized three years later, in 1969. That summer many of the falcon pairs in Cade's study area had stopped nesting, and some of the active nests contained broken eggs or dead nestlings. The dead falcons Cade examined had extremely high pesticide accumulations in their internal organs, and many of the eggs had shells significantly thinner than usual. Cade advised the secretary of the interior about the Peregrine Falcon's dangerous situation. As a result, the bird was placed on the federal Endangered Species List. Cade's research was also a major factor in the banning of DDT in 1972, which required a major effort from scientists, conservationists, and other concerned citizens to accomplish.

When the captive breeding program began in the early 1970s, Cade did not build massive flight cages for the peregrines, hoping to simulate natural conditions. Instead, he attempted to adapt the falcons to living in the breeding chambers constructed for them at Cornell. The birds were taken from wild nests at an early age—usually as tiny, down-covered chicks—and raised specifically to be breeders.

The researchers took many factors—including the falcons' diet and the temperature and length of daylight in their natural environment—into account. They tried to match the hours of light in the breeding chamber with those of the particular pair of falcons' native habitat. They also conducted experiments using artificial insemination, which proved extremely useful for individual falcons that would not reproduce naturally.

Eventually the work paid off. In 1973 The Peregrine Fund produced its first captive-bred falcons—twenty young peregrines. Once they had passed this milestone, the researchers lost no time in attempting to develop new techniques to boost falcon egg production. The most effective proved to be double clutching—taking the first clutch of eggs from a pair of falcons soon after they were laid.

Egg collectors had long known that most birds would re-cycle and lay a second or even a third clutch of eggs if the first ones were destroyed or taken early in the breeding season. Peregrine Fund researchers found that this double-clutching technique worked well with peregrines, and it became a great boon to the falcon recovery program. It was especially valuable for rescuing some of the thin-shelled eggs laid by wild falcons. Many eggs that might have been lost through shell breakage or related problems were successfully hatched in specially humidified incubators.

"By 1975 we had produced enough falcons at our Cornell facility to take the next step—releasing young peregrines into the wild," says Cade. To accomplish this, Peregrine Fund researchers placed young both in traditional nest sites on cliffs and in hack towers—platforms built high above the ground in suitable areas where no natural nest sites existed. Because the young birds had no parents to feed and care for them, field assistants—most of whom were volunteers or received a small stipend—stayed with the birds for several weeks, monitoring their progress and providing fresh meat for them to eat. They avoided letting the young falcons see them when they left their daily rations so the birds would not associate humans with food. After they fledged, the falcons would continue to stay near the release site and accept food until they had learned to hunt for themselves.

This release technique worked well for the most part, although in some locations, with no parents to protect them, the young falcons were killed by other predators. In wilderness areas Great Horned Owls were the single largest cause of death among the newly released falcons, accounting for about 50 percent of all losses in the eastern United States. In the West, Golden Eagles also killed many young peregrines. Some hack-site attendants had the harrowing experience of watching helplessly as young, inexperienced falcons were snatched by these other raptors and carried off to be eaten.

This was a bitter disappointment to The Peregrine Fund's staff and volunteers, who had dreamed of quickly restoring the falcons to the great traditional eyrie cliffs of the East—such as Taughannock Falls here in Ithaca, New York, which Lab founder Arthur "Doc" Allen had taken exquisite photographs of in the 1930s and 1940s. At Taughannock Falls, as at all too many other cliffside release sites in the East, the young peregrines quickly fell victim to owls.

Ask any of the staff and volunteers who took part in those early days of the release program if they ever had any doubts about the future success of the effort, and they'll invariably say no. Failure was unacceptable and, indeed, unimaginable. They just went back and tried again. To counteract the losses experienced at the cliff sites, The Peregrine Fund began releasing young falcons in urban areas, where Golden Eagles and Great Horned Owls would not be a significant threat.

"We decided to try urban releases because the young falcons would be relatively free from predators, and they would have a large supply of food in the form of feral pigeons and starlings," says Cade. "But cities are a mixed blessing. The birds sometimes have problems. They occasionally fly into reflective windows or get into other kinds of trouble. But people do get to see them. It calls attention to the problems of wildlife. The fact that these birds are in cities has created a lot of goodwill for the falcons."

The researchers also hoped that if enough falcons nested in cities to fill up all of the available territories, some birds would eventually disperse away from urban areas and begin reoccupying traditional cliff sites. Indeed, this does appear to be taking place now in a number of areas.

Even prior to the urban releases, however, it was not unheard of for Peregrine Falcons to nest on human-built structures. For centuries the birds have nested on castles in Spain and other areas, and a number of records already existed in the scientific literature of peregrines nesting on bridges and skyscrapers in North America—such as the famous pair that successfully raised young for several years on the Sun Life building in Montreal during the 1950s.

The great milestone year for The Peregrine Fund was 1980. That spring saw the first natural reproduction of Peregrine Falcons east of the Mississippi River in more than twenty years. Three nests produced six young. A modest start, but it was a clear indication of the enormous potential of the program.

And the peregrine recovery's upward momentum continues: The known population of Peregrine Falcons in North America has increased 5 to 10 percent a year since the reintroduction began. Furthermore, no decline in the bird's numbers has been detected in any region of the continent since 1980. The species' numbers in North America have risen meteorically, going from a known breeding population across the continent (excluding Mexico) of 159 nesting pairs in 1975, when the releases began, to 1,539 nesting pairs in 1997, according to the U.S. Fish and Wildlife Service. And these are just the "known" pairs—many more undoubtedly exist. And now the Peregrine Falcon is slated to be removed from the federal Endangered Species List this coming summer.

It's amazing to think back on the early days of the Peregrine Falcon recovery program and realize how much was accomplished in such a relatively short time. More than anything else, the program is a remarkable example of what humans can do to counteract the negative effects our presence has on natural ecosystems. Of course, with DDT being banned in the 1970s, it's possible that the peregrines would eventually have come back on their own—although that is by no means certain. But it definitely would not have happened in our lifetimes, and perhaps not even in those of our children.

Hundreds of Peregrine Falcons now nest across North America from east to west and north to south, and we owe their presence to all the dedicated people who took part in the recovery effort. A remarkable number of them changed the entire direction of their lives to help the peregrines. Some switched careers or took leaves from college to take part. I've never heard anyone say they have any regrets.

As for The Peregrine Fund, the group closed its Cornell facility in the late 1980s as the falcon reintroduction program was nearing completion in the East; it is now headquartered at the World Center for Birds of Prey in Boise, Idaho. Even though The Peregrine Fund's flagship (and namesake) species has successfully recovered, the group has plenty of other vital projects. Threatened raptor species from throughout the world—the California Condor, Mauritius Kestrel, Orange-breasted Falcon, Harpy Eagle, and more—are already being bred in captivity and released by the group to ensure their continued existence, using techniques pioneered for the Peregrine Falcon. And Peregrine Fund researchers have even branched out beyond birds of prey to guide recovery efforts for the 'Alala, the 'Oma'o, and other critically endangered Hawaiian birds. Clearly, they have plenty of work to carry them into the new millennium.

On August 20, 1999, it finally became official: the American Peregrine Falcon was removed from the federal Endangered Species List. Secretary of the Interior Bruce Babbitt made the announcement in Boise, Idaho, at The Peregrine Fund's World Center for Birds of Prey during a gala celebration for the successful recovery of the Peregrine Falcon.

It was a special moment for everyone who took part in the decades-long effort to save this species. I was glad I could attend the two-day celebration, which drew hundreds of people—scientists, former hack-site attendants, falconers, birders, and more—all of whom had worked tirelessly to turn around the peregrine's decline. It was a time to see old friends again and also to meet new people who shared my admiration for the Peregrine Falcon. For me and so many of the staff and volunteers who worked on the peregrine recovery, this experience changed our lives, setting us off in directions we might not otherwise have taken. The road I took eventually led me to The Peregrine Fund's birthplace, the Cornell Laboratory of Ornithology, where I have always tried to promote conservation through our publications.

Was it premature to remove the peregrine from the Endangered Species List? Not if you look at the original goal of the recovery, which was to have 631 pairs of peregrines breeding in North America. According to the latest data, 1,650 breeding pairs exist in the United States and Canada and probably many more in Mexico.

Does the Peregrine Falcon's removal from the Endangered Species List mean that the close monitoring of the bird is over? No; the species will continue to be protected by the Migratory Bird Treaty Act, which prohibits the taking, killing, possession, transportation, and importation of migratory birds, their eggs, parts, and nests except when specifically authorized by the Department of the Interior. In addition, the Endangered Species Act requires a species to be monitored for at least five years after delisting. In the Peregrine Falcon's case, the U.S. Fish and Wildlife Service will monitor the species for thirteen years, conducting population surveys every three years and determining the status of at least two generations of Peregrine Falcons. If during this period the surveys show that the bird needs the full protection of the Endangered Species Act, the Peregrine Falcon will be added to the list again.

9

LAST CHANCE
FOR THE
CALIFORNIA
CONDOR

Spring 1987

The rugged hills spread out below the Bitter Creek overlook have a timeless quality. Shrouded in early-morning fog, they evoke images of primeval earth, where creatures long extinct once eked out a precarious existence, foraging along the deep canyons and slopes of the coastal ranges. Saber-toothed cats, ground sloths, dire wolves—only their bones remain, a dim fossil record of the life-forms that once flourished there.

The condors were there. Long before humans entered this quiet domain the huge birds soared, scouring the land for food. The first human settlers worshiped them as gods—the great thunderbirds. Those who followed were less reverent. After more than a century of persecution—shooting, egg collecting, poisoning—the condors' wild population has been reduced to only two individuals, both male. Now a daring rescue plan devised by the Condor Research Center (CRC) may be all that stands between the condors and extinction.

Headquartered in Ventura, the CRC was set up in 1979 to combat the problem of the condors' precipitous decline. A joint effort of the U.S. Fish and Wildlife Service and the National Audubon Society, the center has been studying the California Condor population and attempting to develop a solution to the birds' dilemma. Examining all the options, condor researchers came to the consensus that captive propagation of the birds was the logical first step. They saw this as the surest way to preserve the condor as a living species and provide young condors for release to the wild.

The plan seemed easy enough on paper: build a breeding population in captivity large enough to sustain the wild population, and eventually to increase it significantly. It had worked with Peregrine Falcons and Whooping Cranes. Why shouldn't it work equally well with California Condors? Indeed, in 1984 prospects seemed bright. Researchers had proved that a condor pair would lay a second and even a third egg in a season if the first egg was taken away from them. The captive population had been boosted to sixteen condors. People were already talking about releasing the first captive-reared condors the following spring. Then the bottom fell out.

During the winter of 1984 four of the five wild breeding pairs of condors were lost. In most cases a single condor showed up, mateless, at the nest site. Although some people believe that the missing birds fled from the area to nest elsewhere as a direct result of research pressure, biologists discount these claims.

"As far as we believe, the missing condors are dead," says Vicky Meretsky, a field biologist with the CRC. "It's very doubtful that they left to nest in other areas. The birds did not vanish in pairs. It was often only one member of a pair that vanished. That's unusual behavior in birds that mate for life."

Hank Pattee, project leader of the CRC, agrees. "It makes no sense to me that an individual bird would leave while its mate stayed," he says. "One pair was manipulated for four years. If there was a negative effect from this, it should have happened in the first year."

All agree that the loss of these breeding condors between the 1984 and 1985 breeding seasons was a major blow to the condor program. "One or two more years of double- and triple-clutching eggs would have given us all the birds we would need for captive breeding," says Pattee.

"The program had been such a huge success up to that point," adds Meretsky. "Just as we appeared to be heading for a turning point, disaster struck. Now we're running a downhill ball game."

The sense of euphoria the researchers felt just two years ago has been replaced with a somber realization that they could fail with the condors. There is now a determination to get the job done as soon as possible. This increased sense of urgency has forced the CRC to revamp its condor recovery program—and to make some difficult, and controversial, decisions. One of the hardest was the decision to trap all the remaining wild condors.

"The staff has been divided from the beginning on this, often quite vocally," says Pattee. The split among the members of the CRC is representative of a much larger division between groups and individuals interested in the condors' well-being. At the heart of the dispute is a philosophical divergence of opinion as to how the condor recovery should be attempted. The members of the CRC favor a hands-on approach—direct intervention in the condors' decline through captive breeding and intense manipulation of the wild population. Conflicts among individual CRC members are concerned only with how far this manipulation should go. Those who favor a hands-off approach, however, believe that the condors should be left alone by humans and that recovery efforts should be centered on more extensive protection and habitat preservation. They are bitterly opposed to trapping the condors.

But any possible negative effects the trapping of the last condors might cause from a public relations standpoint or any schism that might be created among CRC staff members was not taken into consideration. "The decision was made on a purely biological basis," says Pattee.

The need to broaden the condor gene pool was a primary consideration in the decision. With such a small population, a great danger of inbreeding exists, which could result in genetic defects. Bringing the remaining wild condors into the captive breeding pool will help diversify the genetic stock. Moreover, the captive flock has a surplus of female condors, whereas most of the wild condors are males. Capturing them would help even things up and establish more potential breeding pairs.

"It makes no sense to leave the birds out there to die," says Meretsky. "With no female condors present, there is no chance of them breeding in the wild, and they are vitally important as breeding stock." In addition, the mate of one of the wild condors is already in captivity. They were the last California Condors to breed in the wild, and a pair bond is well established between them. It is highly likely that they will breed in captivity.

This decision to capture the remaining condors represents a major restructuring of the condor program's goals. From the start, the purpose of the program was to augment the existing wild condor population through manipulation and captive breeding. Researchers hoped that the wild condors would act as "guide birds" for the captive-bred condors, helping them assimilate into the wild population. This will no longer be a possibility when the last condors are captured, and this is a bitter bone of contention with those who oppose trapping.

As Hank Pattee points out, however, "The wild condor population is so low at this point that the probability of the current wild condors surviving until the young are ready to release is probably nil." And perhaps the use of guide birds would be a negative thing. It could be that the adult condors would only help perpetuate the kinds of feeding habits and behaviors that have led to the condors' present diminished state.

The current scenario for the condor recovery effort is based on research conducted with the Andean Condor—the California Condor's closest relative.

So far the results have been extremely encouraging. Andean Condors are already breeding well in captivity. In fact, there is fast becoming a glut of them.

Because the two species are similar in behavior and physiology, it is logical to believe that California Condors will also breed readily when they reach the proper age. The first birds taken are just reaching breeding age, and one pair is already showing precourtship behavior. According to Pattee, researchers have high hopes that they will lay the first captive-produced California Condor egg this coming spring.

Studies and release programs already carried out with other large vulture species offer hope that their successes can be duplicated with California Condors. Especially encouraging is the work done by Michel Terrasse in central France. Beginning in 1981, Terrasse released European Griffon Vultures into an area where the vultures had been extirpated decades earlier.

Despite the fact that there were no wild Griffon Vultures present to act as guide birds, the released vultures—ranging in age from fledglings to adults— had a low mortality rate. As of 1985, according to Terrasse, more than fifty of the sixty-seven released vultures were alive, and nine pairs laid eggs that year.

The vultures were introduced to the wild using "soft-release" techniques—releasing them gradually from field aviaries over a period of weeks. They were provided amply with carcasses. Though Griffon Vultures are usually long-distance foragers, these birds tended to remain in the area of their release, where abundant food was available. Many of them nested near their release sites. One historic nest cliff was reoccupied a few miles from where the birds were released.

An experimental reintroduction program was also conducted in Peru using Andean Condors. The birds were followed for a year, during which time their range was successfully restricted through feeding programs. During the study period the birds foraged within an area of only a few square miles.

The results of both studies show that under certain circumstances the foraging range of large vultures can be limited. The information gained is directly applicable to the California Condor—which, like the Griffon Vulture and the Andean Condor, is also considered a long-distance forager.

Soft-release techniques and an extensive feeding program could be used to encourage California Condors to stay in safe areas right from the beginning. A plentiful food supply is available in the form of stillborn dairy calves. Because dairy herds are examined regularly by agricultural inspectors, the calves they produce are completely free of contaminants. Moreover, they don't cost anything. Dairy farmers usually must pay to have them hauled away.

Some people are philosophically opposed to regulating the behavior of a species to this extent. They feel that the birds will be somewhat less than the wild and free creatures they were meant to be. The solution to this dilemma should come about naturally in time, provided that sufficient condors exist in the wild. The young captive-bred condors that will later be released will be of the same genetic stock as the last wild ones, and only one generation removed. Natural factors such as competition for nest sites and territories should eventually cause some condors to disperse to other areas. Given a sufficient wild population, the condors should adapt and eventually establish their own balance with their environment.

As Hank Pattee observes, "Ultimately, it is up to the condors what they do after they are released. Right now, we are just trying to save them as a species."

The condor recovery plan calls for the establishment of a stable population of at least twenty-five breeding pairs. To reach this goal, Pattee estimates that there must be one hundred or more condors in the wild. The first releases will most likely take place in the Hudson Ranch area in California, which the U.S. Fish and Wildlife Service purchased earlier this year as a condor refuge. Later, other areas will be selected based on criteria yet to be established. But before any of this happens, a great deal more fieldwork must be done.

As soon as the last wild condor is trapped, the CRC hopes to release a number of Andean Condors in California as part of the research effort. The condors released—ten to twelve in number—will all be females, which will preclude the possibility of a breeding population being established. Each bird will wear a tiny radio transmitter and be followed closely by researchers. The idea is for the field biologists to learn all that they can about reintroducing condors to the wild, using a perfect surrogate species. After two or three years of study, all of the Andean Condors will be recaptured. This will be followed by the release of the first captive-bred California Condors. It is a daring plan, but it holds a great deal of promise.

Probably the biggest problem for the condors in the past has been their inability to bounce back after major population declines. Because they produce only one chick per pair every two years, they do not have sufficient reproductive capability. Thus, early in the twentieth century when the condors were exterminated in Santa Clara and San Luis Obispo counties by specimen collectors, the birds were unable to fill the void.

Vast areas still exist in these and other locations in California that would make excellent condor habitat. The birds simply have not had a sufficient population base to spread into these areas. In many cases, these locations are better than the areas the birds currently occupy.

Condors are creatures of habit and tend in most cases to frequent the breeding and foraging grounds where they were raised. One positive development in the reintroduction program could be to release condors in the lost areas of their former range—areas carefully determined to meet the necessary criteria. Numerous ideal locations exist in the Sierra Nevada, on both the eastern and western slopes. Offshore islands also offer promising areas. All that is necessary is for the captive breeding program to provide enough young condors. With double- and triple-clutching of eggs, researchers feel this should not be a problem.

For now, however, all that researchers can do is wait for the captive condors to breed, and continue their efforts to capture the last wild birds. They have been besieged recently by individuals, groups, journalists, and television crews asking to be there when the last wild condor is trapped. Hank Pattee finds their sudden deep interest difficult to understand.

"Personally, I don't want to be there when the last condor is trapped," he says. "I want to be there when the first captive-bred California Condor is released."

10

ALOFT AGAIN

Autumn 1991

Ap29 19, 1987, is a date that biologist Pete Bloom will never forget. On that quiet Easter Sunday morning, Bloom lay buried in a pit blind in the rugged hills of the Los Padres National Forest, watching as the last free-flying California Condor inched closer and closer to a stillborn calf sprawled on the ground nearby. The condor, an adult male called AC-9 (Adult Condor 9), was wary. During the previous six months he had seen the few other remaining wild condors trapped one by one—either snared in a fifty-square-foot cannon net shot over the bird or grabbed directly by someone hiding underground in one of the cramped boxes known as pit blinds. The great bird peered from side to side and then bent toward the dead calf, stretching his neck to full extension to reach the food. At that instant Bloom triggered the cannon net. The bird lurched away, trying to outrun the net, but it was too late.

Bloom's satisfaction at a job well done was already tinged with sorrow as he carefully folded the wings of the last wild California Condor. "Trapping

AC-9 was the most incredible experience I've ever had," says Bloom. "In some ways, it was both the high point and the low point of my life. I was hired principally to capture condors, so trapping the last one was certainly the highlight of my career. But it was also sad. I knew that for the first time in thousands of years there were no California Condors left in the air. I think all of us who were there that day had mixed emotions."

Nearly five years have passed since Pete Bloom trapped AC-9. For some people, that event marked the final chapter in the saga of a species that had flown above the North American continent for millennia, dating back to a time when mastodons and saber-toothed cats still roamed the earth. They believed the California Condor was extinct as a wild species and would probably stay that way. But recent events may provide a second chance at freedom for this colossal vulture. Thanks to the captive breeding efforts of the Los Angeles Zoo and the San Diego Wild Animal Park, the number of California Condors has nearly doubled—from the twenty-seven birds alive in 1987 to a total of fifty-three at the end of the 1991 breeding season.

And this past June the Condor Recovery Team—an advisory group set up to guide condor population enhancement efforts—asked the U.S. Fish and Wildlife Service to authorize the release of two California Condor chicks by the end of the year. It was a significant moment for team leader Lloyd Kiff. "I signed the recommendation to bring the birds into captivity five years ago," he says. "And now I just got through signing the recommendation for the California Condor reintroduction to begin. I'm glad that I could be team leader long enough to bridge that gap." According to Kiff, if all goes as planned, two young California Condors will be soaring free above their native range by this coming winter.

This happy scenario provides hope for birders, ornithologists, and anyone else who would be filled with awe at the sight of a flying condor. Perhaps we *can* still turn around the California Condor's decline. But how did these magnificent birds ever reach their precarious condition in the first place? Actually, the condors' problems began long before the present century. During the Pleistocene epoch, some eleven thousand years ago, condors were widespread. Fossil remains of the birds dating from that period have been found from the West Coast of North America all the way east to what are now the states of New York and Florida. As many large mammals—giant sloths, mastodons—died off and finally became extinct, the condors lost a major food source. Their range shrank considerably. By the time the Spaniards visited the New World in the late fifteenth century, condors were already primarily a West Coast species.

Centuries later, thanks to the California gold rush of 1849, the birds faced another serious threat. Thousands of would-be miners flooded into the state, and most of them owned guns. The large, slow-moving condors provided an irresistible target. Numerous letters and diaries of the Old West tell of shooting "giant buzzards." California Condors were also killed by scientists and collectors in the late nineteenth and early twentieth centuries.

A more prolific species might have been able to absorb the losses from shooting. Condors, however, take five or six years to reach breeding age, and in the wild they generally raise only one chick every two years. The premature deaths of numerous adult condors placed an unbearable strain on their population.

By the time a serious effort to save the species was launched in the 1980s, the condors were already well on their way toward extinction. The situation called for drastic measures. Researchers decided to increase condor surveillance to determine the major causes of the birds' decline, to manipulate the wild birds through multiple clutching so that they would produce more eggs, and to take some condors into captivity to use as breeders whose offspring could later be released.

The condor recovery looked like an unqualified success during the early 1980s. The number of known wild breeding pairs was steadily increasing—three pairs in 1981 and 1982, four in 1983, and five in 1984. The captive population had grown to sixteen condors. The Condor Recovery Team had plans to start releasing captive-reared birds to augment the wild population. Then came the 1984–85 crash of the wild condor population and the subsequent decision to capture all remaining wild California Condors.

This decision unleashed a storm of controversy within the conservation community. Even scientists directly involved with manipulating the condors were split over the issue. The symbolism of capturing the last free-flying California Condors obviously troubled people who had such a strong commitment to the birds' well-being. But state and federal agencies eventually gave the go-ahead, and within a few months the remaining wild condors joined the captive flock.

The controversy over condor trapping died down somewhat as recovery efforts moved from the field to the breeding facilities at the Los Angeles Zoo and the San Diego Wild Animal Park. Then, on March 3, 1988, less than a year after Pete Bloom brought in the last wild condor, a pair of California Condors at the San Diego facility laid the first captive-produced egg—a major milestone for the program and the species. Molloko, a female condor chick, hatched on April 29.

Since then, egg production has increased steadily each spring, though not all of the eggs have been fertile. In 1989 four chicks hatched from seven eggs; in 1990 eight chicks hatched from fifteen eggs laid. This past spring was the best to date, with thirteen chicks hatched from twenty-two eggs. The total California condor population now stands at fifty-three birds, up from twenty-seven in 1987.

"I expect condor egg production to plateau for two or three years in the neighborhood of twenty-five to thirty eggs a year," says Bill Toone, curator of birds at the San Diego Wild Animal Park. "After that, the birds that hatched in 1988, 1989, and 1990 should start breeding and boost the numbers even higher."

Some condor pairs are now producing two and even three eggs per season—a remarkable increase for the species. People sometimes ask whether pushing the condors to this level of egg production could eventually discourage them from breeding. Toone is doubtful. "We do it with many other birds," he says. "People keep talking about birds losing interest in breeding, but they seldom take all of the variables into account. Birds in the wild often lose their eggs, but they usually attempt to lay again."

Toone points out that ravens frequently destroyed California Condor eggs in the wild. Sometimes a pair would lay two or three eggs and still not be able to raise a chick because of such predation. "I think that the birds have evolved around the necessity of having to deal with the loss of their eggs," he says.

A much more insidious threat in Toone's opinion is the possibility that future generations of condors will have reproductive problems associated with inbreeding. Perhaps the decline went too far and now too few condors exist to provide the genetic diversity necessary to sustain a species.

"A number of birds are old enough but have not bred yet," says Toone. "Why haven't they? We have some birds that are breeders and yet lay abnormal eggs with low hatchability. These are just the kinds of reproductive problems that are typical of inbreeding."

Mike Wallace, curator of birds at the Los Angeles Zoo, has similar fears. "I feel comfortable with the way we've worked out the breeding in captivity and also the release techniques," he says, "but the real question is genetic. It will take several decades before we really know whether or not the species has a long-term future." Both Wallace and Toone agree that the only reasonable hope is to produce as many condors as possible.

Maintaining genetic diversity in the condor flock has been a major consideration from the start of the captive breeding program. Researchers took blood samples from the condors and compared their DNA characteristics to determine which birds should be put together to form pairs. They tried to avoid pairing up closely related birds.

One of the major obstacles in the way of early California Condor releases has been the need to ensure that each condor bloodline is adequately represented in the captive flock. The Recovery Team requires that a condor pair must produce at least five young to add to the captive flock before any of their offspring can be released. This condition has now been met.

Three release candidates—one from the San Diego Wild Animal Park and the others from the Los Angeles Zoo—have been chosen, though only two of them will actually be set free. "We decided to be conservative this time," says Toone. "Next year we'll probably be able to do a more ample release of California Condors, perhaps as many as six."

The Condor Recovery Team had originally stipulated that at least three condors would be released at a time. (Researchers believe that the birds' physical and social development is enhanced if they are raised in a group of three or more.) To make up the desired group number, two young Andean Condors will be set free with the California Condors.

If the U.S. Fish and Wildlife Service gives the expected go-ahead, the birds will be taken to a cliffside release site at the Sespe Condor Refuge in southern California, probably this coming October when they are approximately five months old. There the condors will be placed in a roost box measuring twelve feet by eight feet by six feet high. This prefabricated structure has insulated walls to provide protection during harsh weather, and also a blind attached to the side so that researchers can observe the condors without being seen. The condors will be able to go out into a large, net-covered area where they can sun themselves, exercise their wings, and get used to their surroundings.

When the youngest bird is eight months old—in late December or January—the netting will be removed, and for the first time in nearly five years a California Condor will have the chance to spread its wings and soar. It is an eagerly awaited event.

"I'm really looking forward to getting those birds out there again," says David Clendenen, lead condor field biologist. Clendenen has spent much of the past nine years of his life working with the condors—long enough to have experienced the euphoria of the early 1980s, when it seemed that nothing could go wrong, and also the despair of 1984, when the birds' wild population plummeted. He personally helped trap some of the last wild condors.

"It's been a long road, and I'm getting tired," he says. "But I made a vow to myself that I would be here until the California Condors are out in the wild again, and I intend to keep it."

Clendenen and the rest of the release team are more than adequately prepared for this momentous step in the recovery program. For more than two years the field biologists have been experimenting with condor release techniques, using captive-bred Andean Condors in the Los Padres National Forest—an area where wild California Condors still flew until 1987. Thirteen birds have been set free in four separate releases since 1988, when the program began.

The Andean Condor release program has had a twofold purpose: to experiment with release techniques that will later be used with California Condors and also to train an effective field crew. Fieldwork with the surrogate birds has already yielded valuable data. Some of the plans for future California Condor reintroduction efforts have been modified based on this research. The field biologists had originally hoped to encourage the condors to stay in a relatively small, safe area by providing abundant food—techniques that had worked well with released Griffon Vultures in France. It was a different story with the Andean Condors. The birds ranged far from the release area, some traveling more than a hundred miles from the feeding site. On the positive side, however, the birds returned to the site when they were hungry.

Some biologists believe that feeding on contaminated food—particularly the remains of shot deer containing lead bullet fragments—was a major cause of mortality in the wild condor population. By providing most or all of the wild condors' food in the form of stillborn dairy calves, researchers hope that they can greatly reduce the threat from lead poisoning.

The calf carcasses are set out at feeding sites in the rugged peaks of the Los Padres National Forest. The idea is to teach the birds to forage only in remote areas, far from human interference. "The birds are shy about going down to a new spot," says Wallace. "If we can get them used to feeding only on the mountaintops, they should become reluctant to go down and land on the flats."

Wallace—who pioneered release techniques with Black Vultures and Turkey Vultures in Florida and with Andean Condors in Peru—designed the California Condor release program. He is not disappointed in how the released birds have reacted. "The main goal of the release program was to have some kind of control over the birds' eating, and we're finding that it's doing just that," he says. "They're feeding right at the areas where we want them to. It's fine if they fly off a hundred miles or so. If they'll do that and stay up in the peaks away from people, then we've got a program."

All of the Andean Condors from the initial release in 1988 have been recaptured and are slated to be released in Colombia, South America, as part of an effort to reintroduce the birds in an area where they have been extirpated. Four Andean Condors from last year's release still fly free over the Sespé Condor Sanctuary, though they may be trapped before the California Condor releases begin.

Despite all the worries associated with the condor program (Is the wild environment too hazardous for them? Will genetic problems prove insurmountable?), most of the researchers involved with the California Condor Recovery Program are hopeful about the eventual outcome. They plan to establish two or more disjunct populations of a hundred condors—one of them in the birds' last stronghold in Southern California. Other release sites being considered are Arizona's Grand Canyon and the Gray Ranch, a 321,000-acre property in New Mexico owned by The Nature Conservancy.

Though some California Condors may eventually disperse, setting up territories and foraging without human assistance, the bulk of their population will be intensively managed for the foreseeable future. As Mike Wallace says, "It has to be a managed situation. We can't just let them live off our garbage, which is what they've been doing for the last one hundred years. That's why they're dying. We've got to take responsibility: create a space for the condors, find out what their needs are, and modify human behavior to accommodate the birds. That's what it will take if we are going to have wild California Condors in the next century."

Much has happened in the years since I wrote these two essays on the California Condor. The total population of this species now numbers 160, but what's most exciting is that 49 of them are in the wild in California and Arizona and an additional 10 are in field pens being prepared for release.

Unfortunately, the reintroduction efforts haven't gone as smoothly as many researchers had hoped. Some of the released birds were killed in mishaps. At least three died in collisions with power lines. One died from ingesting antifreeze, and several others died of lead poisoning from feeding on deer carcasses riddled with bullet fragments. Some released condors were far too unafraid of humans and had to be retrapped. Researchers had to develop aversion training techniques to discourage dangerous behavior in the condors. In the condor flight pens, for example, they set up dummy utility poles that would give the birds a mild shock if they landed on them.

Another California Condor captive breeding facility was added in 1993 when The Peregrine Fund built breeding chambers for the birds at its World Center for Birds of Prey in Boise, Idaho. Now all three facilities are producing young condors for release.

The reintroduction effort took a major step forward on December 12, 1996, when six young captive-bred condors—five from the Los Angeles Zoo and one from the World Center for Birds of Prey—were set free at the Vermilion Cliffs in northern Arizona. This was the first time condors had been released outside of California. Sixty miles north of the Grand Canyon, the area is remote and—with 40 miles of vertical cliff face averaging 1,000 feet or more in height—it's a superb place for young condors to perfect their flying.

But one of the most important events so far in the condor recovery took place just as we were going through the final proofreading of this book. On March 25, 2001, a pair of released California Condors laid an egg at a nest in Arizona's Grand Canyon. (Before this, the last egg produced in the wild was laid in 1986.) The female condor had been hatched in March 1995 and was released at the Vermilion Cliffs site with eight other condors in May 1997.

Although the egg was since inadvertently broken by the adult condors, the significance of this pair having laid it cannot be overstated. At six years old, California Condors are just reaching breeding age, so this is the earliest that this female could have been expected to produce an egg. And young condors are notoriously clumsy during their initial nesting attempts. With more experience and maturity, the breeding success ratio of this and other pairs can only improve. This pair may even produce another egg this season. So it's possible—and perhaps even probable—that we will see California Condors once again reproducing in the wild within the next two or three years.

11
THE EAGLES
RETURN

June 1987

There is an indisputable majesty about the Bald Eagle. Large and powerful, beautiful to behold, it is an appropriate symbol of the nation. Unfortunately, in many parts of the Bald Eagle's former range, the birds have dwindled or vanished altogether.

Such was the case with Santa Catalina, a picturesque island twenty-five miles off the Southern California coast. Once relatively common there, the Bald Eagle plummeted in numbers during the early twentieth century, a victim of hunting, egg collecting, environmental contamination, and other forms of intrusion into the island's delicate ecosystem. Until recently no Bald Eagles had attempted to nest there since the 1940s. Now, thanks to an intensive eagle release program, Bald Eagles can once more be seen hunting along the coast or perched on the high cliffs of Santa Catalina Island.

Since the Bald Eagle Restoration Project began in 1980, the Institute for Wildlife Studies, headed by Dave Garcelon, has released thirty-three eagles on Catalina. The birds were taken as seven- to nine-week-old nestlings from areas in the Pacific Northwest with abundant Bald Eagle populations. They were raised on hack towers—elevated platforms where they can be fed without seeing humans—in a remote area of Catalina Island.

The eagles were provided with food until they became proficient at hunting for themselves. All of the eagles released this past spring—eight in number—are now self-sufficient, existing mostly on fish they catch along the coast of the island.

At least eighteen of the original thirty-three eagles released are still surviving and accounted for on the island—six adults and twelve immatures. Fifty percent survivability in a wild population is considered good, so in a program of this kind the ratio is excellent. And some of the missing eagles may still be alive and could possibly return to the island at some point.

"We've had a few birds show up in the past two years that we didn't even know were still around," says Dave Garcelon. "It shows that some of the eagles are moving to places we don't know about and then coming back to Catalina as adults."

Although one of the eagle pairs built a nest in 1984, this past spring was the first time that an egg was actually laid by one of the released birds. The eagles built a nest barely ten feet above the ground in a tiny Catalina cherry tree. They incubated the egg for thirteen days, but unfortunately, it broke. Even though the egg didn't hatch, Garcelon feels that a great deal of progress is being made by the project.

"That was the first Bald Eagle egg laid on the Channel Islands in more than forty years," he says. "It's a really long process when you work with such long-lived birds. Bald Eagles don't even mature fully until they're five or six years old, and then it may take a few years for them to get established as breeders."

The restoration project on Santa Catalina is providing an unparalleled opportunity for long-term eagle study. Because the island is relatively small and isolated and has a plentiful supply of prey, few of the eagles venture off the island.

"Very few programs have the breadth to be able to follow eagles both on their nesting grounds and in their wintering areas," says Garcelon. "We have the opportunity to look at the same individual eagles on a year-round basis."

The short-term goal of the restoration project was just to find out whether the eagles would survive and stay on the island. That goal has certainly been met. But the ultimate goal is to establish a self-sustaining Bald Eagle population on Catalina. Perhaps if enough young eagles are produced there by the released birds, Bald Eagles may also move back into other areas of their former range, such as nearby San Clemente Island.

So far the high point of the restoration project for Dave Garcelon was when he began seeing Bald Eagles in full adult plumage on the island.

"I could finally see what a difference the project was making when I saw adult eagles out there," he says. "That was the climax of all the work for me. I'd followed these birds from when they were fuzzy things in a nest. All of a sudden they were flying around as adult eagles and trying to reproduce. They had gone full cycle."

12

DESERT FALCON

Summer 1989

Few things are as awesome to see as a large falcon in flight. The ability to climb quickly to a lofty altitude and the amazing speed of a falcon's power dive or stoop are unsurpassed in nature. Though when most people think of falcons, the Peregrine Falcon probably comes to mind, in the western states there lives another superb raptor every bit as impressive: the Prairie Falcon.

A quintessential desert falcon, the Prairie Falcon is uniquely adapted to survive in a harsh, arid environment. Their pale brown backs and creamy white breasts spotted with brown allow these falcons to blend in well with the typical desert habitat of the American West. Their preferred hunting methods—low-level patrols or long-distance, high-speed sneak attacks from high perches—are also well suited for the wide expanses of open or semi-open land the birds frequent.

Prairie Falcons must be admired for their ability to eke out an existence in an inhospitable environment. Versatile hunters, they will readily switch to feeding on various lizards, rodents, and even insects if birds are scarce.

The similarity in size between a Prairie Falcon and the slightly larger Peregrine Falcon make comparisons inevitable. Actually, however, a number of significant differences exist between the two species in terms of appearance, habitat needs, and hunting styles.

Most birders would probably agree that Prairie Falcons are not quite as striking to look at as peregrines. They lack the large, dark facial markings that often form a full "cap" on an adult Peregrine Falcon. Instead, they have only small, narrow "mustache marks" on the sides of their head. Their bodies are more tubular and their tails longer than those of the peregrine. Prairie Falcons' most distinctive features in flight are the dark axillaries and coverts on the underside of their wings, which show up as dark triangles in the distance. No other North American falcon shares this field mark.

Prairie Falcons do not go through a spectacular plumage change during their first molt—unlike peregrines, which change from dark brown or black on their backs to deep blue. It's often difficult to distinguish between a juvenile and an adult Prairie Falcon unless you can get a good view through a spotting scope. The adults tend to be pale cream-white below, spotted with brown. The feet and cere (the fleshy covering around the nostrils) are usually yellow or orange in older birds. Juvenile Prairie Falcons tend to be a buffy color below with brown streaks. Their feet and cere usually lack the color of an adult bird, at least through most of their first year.

Peregrines are generally found in lush areas, often along rivers, lakes, marshes, or coastlines. They have a quite aerial hunting style, often hurtling down at prey from an impressive altitude or engaging in long high-altitude tail-chases. They live virtually entirely on birds, ranging in size from small passerines to large waterfowl.

Prairie Falcons sometimes hunt in a style similar to that of peregrines, but it is not their usual method. More often, they will sit on a high perch—a rocky outcropping or a man-made object such as a utility pole—scanning the ground for perhaps miles around. When a Prairie Falcon spies prey in a good setup for attack, it will drop from its perch and fly at high speed, often barely above the ground, using the natural contours of the landscape to mask its approach. When it reaches the prey, it will attempt either to rake it on the ground—especially if it is a terrestrial animal such as a lizard or a ground squirrel—or snatch it just as it takes off.

Often a flock of Horned Larks or other small open-country birds will burst into the air before a falcon has reached them. But with the momentum it has built up during its high-speed approach, the falcon can often pick off a small bird before it reaches adequate escape speed.

Prairie Falcons generally choose high cliffs for their nest sites (although I have found a couple of unusually low eyries in areas with a high density of prey and a shortage of good cliffs). As with most birds of prey, the female Prairie Falcon is substantially larger—about one-third more in size and weight—than the male. The courtship display is impressive, with the male putting on an awesome show of high flying and stooping that is breathtaking to watch. He will also bring food to his potential mate, exhibiting his prowess as a hunter.

Prairie Falcons do not construct a nest as such. The female lays her eggs, three to five in number, in a simple scrape made in the soft sand on the bottom of a ledge or pothole. Sometimes Prairie Falcons nest in stick nests on desert cliffs, but they are invariably using the abandoned nest of a raven, hawk, or other nest builder.

Both sexes share in the incubation, which lasts between twenty-nine and thirty-three days. The down-covered young are completely helpless at birth. It is amazing to see the care and delicacy these fierce predators show in the care and feeding of their tiny young.

The male does most of the hunting to support the brood, and it is quite a chore at times. As the young grow larger, they stand at the edge of their nest ledge, screaming loudly and shaking their wings to attract attention whenever an adult comes into view. The nestlings generally fledge within seven weeks of hatching.

Prairie Falcons are highly territorial, both around their nest sites and in their wintering areas. They will readily attack and drive off birds much larger than themselves, such as Golden Eagles. The birds usually put on a spectacular show when they harass another raptor, making impressive vertical dives as they chase the intruder out of the territory.

Prairie Falcons make no migration as such, though many will leave their breeding territories and move into other areas in winter. I usually start looking for them in early fall around agricultural areas in the desert. Alfalfa fields seem to be a favorite haunt. This low-cut, well-watered crop provides habitat for grassland bird species and their predators. Utility poles that carry power lines to irrigation pumps and other farm equipment provide excellent perches from which to launch surprise attacks.

Whenever I'm birding around alfalfa farms in the desert, I always make a point of stopping to check the crosspieces of utility poles with my binoculars. You'd be surprised how often an "insulator" turns out to be a Prairie Falcon. If you do spot a falcon perched on a pole, it's best to keep a good distance away, watching with binoculars or a spotting scope. Prairie Falcons are relatively spooky and will fly away if you get too close. If you wait out a perched falcon, however, chances are you'll see it make an attack.

The Prairie Falcon is one of the most fascinating of North America's raptors. If you are lucky enough to live within its range—virtually the entire West from southern Canada down into Mexico—make a point of searching out this remarkable bird. If you spot one in action, you're sure to see a dazzling display of aerial virtuosity.

13
HOME ON THE RANGE

Summer 1989

The angry scream of an adult female Prairie Falcon drifting out from the nesting cliff is the first sign of trouble. Even from our distant vantage point more than two hundred yards away and across the wide Bow River, her call is loud and harsh. A quick scan downriver with binoculars reveals the cause of the falcon's anxiety—a Golden Eagle is flying toward the falcon eyrie.

The falcon bursts from the cliff with a visible fury, screaming as she circles upward in tight circles to get above the eagle. As soon as she reaches her position, more than one thousand feet high, she turns down and with a few quick pumps of her wings hurtles meteorlike toward the larger bird.

Just as a pile-driving impact seems inevitable, the eagle rolls over in midair and raises its enormous feet toward the falcon. The falcon pulls up from the dive, allowing her momentum to carry her back to a position nearly as high as her original pitch. She repeats the dive again and again, harrying the eagle until the bird turns away from the falcon eyrie and drifts back toward its own nest, only a mile downstream.

The skirmish between the two birds is part of an age-old battle—a territorial imperative to keep the area surrounding a nest as danger-free as possible. A Golden Eagle is a very real threat to a Prairie Falcon. These eagles, like most predators, are opportunists and will snatch young falcons from their nest ledges if they have a chance. Only the constant vigil of the falcons can ensure the safety of their brood.

Now that the falcon's dazzling display of aerial virtuosity is over, we set down our binoculars and reach for our notebooks. Larry O'Brien, the field assistant I accompanied to the falcon eyrie, jots down a few quick notes in the terse language of a researcher: "1800 hours: adult female chases Golden Eagle from nest area." It is a brief notation, but when added to the notes O'Brien and the others have made during their many hours spent observing the Bow River Prairie Falcons, it becomes an important addition to a body of data that may help ensure the continued survival of the falcons on the prairies of southern Alberta, Canada.

The eyrie we are watching is one of four Prairie Falcon nests that Canadian Wildlife Service biologists have been monitoring as part of a three-year study aimed at documenting the effects of increased agricultural development on prairie grasslands. The researchers hope to find ways to bring agricultural practices into harmony with the needs of wildlife on the prairie. Studying the Prairie Falcon is a first step on the way to that goal.

"The study is basically a Prairie Falcon/agriculture integration project," says Geoffrey Holroyd, the leader of the project. "We're trying to use Prairie Falcons as an indicator of dry-land conditions adjacent to rivers."

On the vast prairies of southern Alberta, Prairie Falcons are restricted almost entirely to nesting along rivers. The birds are cliff nesters and, in this part of the country, the only suitable cliffs available are the dirt cutbanks carved into the rolling hills by rivers.

If this study indicates that a raptor like a Prairie Falcon can serve as an effective indicator of the health of grassland ecosystems along a river, then biologists will conduct similar research using other birds of prey—Ferruginous Hawks, Swainson's Hawks, Burrowing Owls—that are not limited to riparian nesting habitat.

The Prairie Falcon is an excellent species for the study at hand. Although the birds are still relatively common breeders in the Bow River study area, they have suffered a major decline in their Alberta range during the past thirty years.

In the early 1960s the birds' breeding area extended north all the way to the city of Edmonton, in central Alberta. Now the Red Deer River, more than one hundred miles south of Edmonton, is the northernmost limit of their breeding range.

Researchers assume that this decline in range is directly attributable to the displacement of grassland habitats by farms and woodlands. The hard evidence to prove this point is lacking at present, but the researchers on the falcon project are interested in whether they can document a correlation between the intensity of agricultural development and environmental stresses on the birds.

Holroyd's Bow River study area is centered near the town of Scandia, Alberta. The area is a unique blend of plowed farmland and rangeland, used for cattle grazing. Though it is widely farmed, high spots of land and rolling hills in some areas are difficult to irrigate and are not plowed. Approximately 50 percent of the study area still consists of native prairie grassland.

"Because of its mosaic of habitats, the area is almost ideal in terms of looking at how different pairs are foraging in the different land-use areas," says Holroyd.

The four nest sites in the study were carefully selected to take advantage of the area's unique qualities. Two of the nests are immediately adjacent to agricultural lands, whereas the others are next to prairie rangeland. During the course of the three-year study, the researchers should be able to document whether a significant difference exists between the hunting and nesting success of rangeland-nesting falcons and that of farmland-nesting pairs.

The study area near Scandia also has other qualities that make it a good research location: It has a relatively large Prairie Falcon population, and it was the site of another raptor study conducted by the Canadian Wildlife Service in the early 1970s. Ursula Banasch, who is working on the current project, helped with the original surveys conducted by Richard Fyfe, who is now retired. Using both the existing and the newly acquired data, the researchers will be able to compare the past and present ratio of nesting success in this area to detect any declines in nest productivity.

According to Banasch, the original falcon studies were concerned primarily with the endangered Peregrine Falcon—a species that vanished from the area as a breeder in the 1970s due to environmental contamination by DDT and other pesticides.

The two species had coexisted together along some Alberta rivers in the past. Peregrines feed primarily on birds, and they absorbed high concentrations of the pesticide by consuming insect-eating birds. The Alberta Prairie Falcons escaped most of the negative effects of pesticides, however, because they prefer to feed on ground squirrels—a relatively pesticide-free prey. But now the Prairie Falcons' dependence on these squirrels may, ironically, lead to their demise. Ground squirrel populations are being devastated by agriculture. Farmers plow up the squirrel burrows when they're preparing to plant their crops. They also set out poison to kill the squirrels that persist. These practices have drastically reduced the number of ground squirrels available for falcons to hunt, and of course the abundance of prey is a key factor in the nesting success of a falcon pair.

If you spend enough time in the field observing nesting falcons, you begin to see the importance of the connection between the birds and their prey. Early in the season while the falcons are incubating eggs, you see few ground squirrels on the Alberta prairie—just an occasional full-grown adult sitting close to its burrow. But by the time the falcon eggs hatch, a sudden blossoming of the ground squirrel population takes place, with young squirrels emerging from burrows all across the prairie.

The young ground squirrels immediately become the major prey for most large grassland raptors, and the Prairie Falcons' nest cycle is timed perfectly to take advantage of this abundant food source. We can only speculate what might happen if ground squirrels were to disappear completely from the falcons' breeding grounds.

To gather the data needed to document the effects of agriculture on Prairie Falcons, you must spend long hours in the field during spring and summer, observing the nesting birds in action. At each nest site researchers observe the adult falcons' hunting behavior. They record the distances traveled to forage, the success ratio of the hunts, the number of young fledged from successful falcon nests, and other pertinent information.

Each adult falcon in the study area is captured and fitted with a small radio transmitter to facilitate tracking the movements of the birds as they hunt. The miniature transmitters are attached to the bird's two central tail feathers, but because they are lightweight and small, they don't impair the behavior of a falcon or its ability to fly.

The work begins in earnest after the transmitters are installed. Observers monitor each eyrie, and mobile teams attempt to track the hunting falcons with radio receivers. Each handheld receiver has a directional antenna that receives a pulsating *beep* signal, which is loudest when the antenna is pointing directly toward the bird. By getting cross-references with two or more receivers, it is possible to pinpoint the location of a given bird with a fair degree of accuracy. Each falcon transmitter has its own frequency, which makes identifying the individual birds simple.

The biologists use walkie-talkies to keep in contact with each other. It is amazing how well the observations come together when researchers use telemetry. One person calls from the eyrie to report that an adult falcon has left the nest and is flying due north. A couple of minutes later someone to the north picks up the signal—and perhaps even spots the bird flying past. Soon the adult is tracked as it returns to the nest, carrying prey. The nest observer identifies the type of prey, and all the observations add up to form an accurate picture of where the birds are hunting most and where they are most successful.

The information collected during the first year of the project indicates that foraging is more difficult for falcons nesting adjacent to cultivated areas. One female Prairie Falcon from such an area flew eight miles away to hunt, then had to lug a ground squirrel—which weighs fully half as much as a falcon—all the way back to her nest. Conversely, the researchers saw some of the range-land-nesting falcons making successful hunts within sight of their eyries. It is too early to say what this means in terms of nesting success, but if the adult falcons are having difficulty foraging to feed their young, this is bound to create stress that may result in lower productivity.

If the research project shows that falcons nesting in farming areas are consistently less successful in producing and caring for young than falcons nesting on prairie rangeland, scientists will have solid data to show the detrimental effects that agricultural development has on Prairie Falcons.

But Holroyd insists that he is not trying to gather evidence that will be used to block farming projects. What he really would like to do is to find ways that farmers can alter their agricultural practices to help wildlife without harming their own livelihoods in any way.

"Agriculture is here to say," says Holroyd. "We all have to eat, and farming provides a major source of foreign export funds for the Canadian economy. We must find a way to help agriculture meet its needs and also accommodate wildlife."

Holroyd has found a great deal of acceptance for his project among range managers, farmers, and other pro-agriculture groups.

"The indication I've had so far from some of the land management agencies and farmers is that they're hungry for this material," he notes. "They want literature telling them how to incorporate wildlife into their plans. They're eager to use farming techniques that will help out wildlife, so long as they can still make a living."

According to Holroyd, the primary goal of the study is to integrate the habitat needs of Prairie Falcons into the current and future land-use practices of southern Alberta. The information gained can then also be used with other species in other regions, in Canada and abroad. Holroyd believes that it is vitally important to get the information out to the farmers and hear their feedback. In fall 1991 he intends to make the rounds of the agricultural community, telling farmers exactly what conclusions the researchers have reached based on the study and discussing ideas and recommendations that the farmers can incorporate into their agricultural practices.

"We plan to talk with the federal and provincial agencies that advise farmers and also to the farmers themselves," says Holroyd. "We need their feedback to make sure our ideas are realistic. If they're not, then we may need to reevaluate everything and work in another direction. But we'll need their input to be sure.

"We can do this study and publish it in a scientific journal," he concludes, "but it won't be worth a plugged nickel if we can't get it out to the landowners to use."

14

OPEN-COUNTRY
HUNTER

Summer 1989

The scientific name of the Ferruginous Hawk—*Buteo regalis*—is certainly appropriate for this most regal of North American hawks. Larger and stronger than a Red-tailed Hawk, with legs feathered to the toes like a Golden Eagle, a white breast and tail, and striking rust-colored accents on its thighs and back, the Ferruginous Hawk is stunning.

Ferruginous means "rust colored" and refers to the splashes of that color on the light-phase birds. The dark-phase Ferruginous Hawks, which are much less common than light-phase, are uniformly dark on their bodies, except for their tails and flight feathers. The two color phases do not represent distinct subspecies. They freely interbreed, and some nests contain offspring of both color phases.

Unlike Red-tailed Hawks and many other North American buteos, which have greater leeway in the types of habitats in which they can exist, the

Ferruginous Hawk is a habitat specialist. The birds are almost always associated with grasslands—primarily short-grass prairie and rangeland. In some parts of their range, such as in northern Alberta, where woodlands are spreading south and encroaching on traditional prairie areas, this hawk's range is decreasing.

Ferruginous Hawks nest on the vast open lands of the prairie in the north-central and western states of the United States and the prairie provinces of Canada. During the harsh northern winter, the birds usually move to similar grasslands in places such as Texas and southern California, far to the south.

Ferruginous Hawks are also specialists when it comes to diet. Studies have shown that the Ferruginous Hawks west of the Rocky Mountains live almost entirely on jackrabbits during the nesting season, whereas the eastern birds—nesting in Montana, the Dakotas, and into Canada—consume mostly ground squirrels.

According to Josef Schmutz, a noted Canadian raptor researcher, Richardson's ground squirrels make up 90 percent or more of the diets of the Ferruginous Hawks nesting in his study area in the province of Alberta. He has been able to document in a remarkable way how directly the growth and decline of the Ferruginous Hawk population is tied with similar fluctuations in the ground squirrel population.

By examining purchase records for ground squirrel poison used by farmers in past years, Schmutz showed a paradoxical correlation between the increased use of squirrel poison and increases in the Ferruginous Hawk population. Not that the poison itself helps the hawks in any way; instead, an increase in the use of poison reflects a major upswing in the number of squirrels present in a given area. In boom years for squirrels the Ferruginous Hawk population showed a corresponding upswing in numbers.

"We looked at the amount of poison used by landowners and it paralleled the rise in the Ferruginous Hawk population quite nicely," says Schmutz. "As of 1986, we have had a significant rise in Ferruginous Hawk numbers. That was the same year that poison use shot up. We assume that it reflects a change in ground squirrel density."

The farmers unwittingly accomplished some important research, providing valuable squirrel population data for past seasons. When biologists attempt to determine approximate ground squirrel numbers in a given area, they usually conduct random burrow counts. The farmers performed the equivalent of a burrow count, walking along the edges of their fields and putting out poison whenever they found a ground squirrel burrow. The more burrows they found, the more poison they used.

Schmutz also noticed that the average number of young in Ferruginous Hawk nests increased in years when more poison was used, again reflecting a ground squirrel population increase. With such evidence as this, it's easy to see how specialized the hawks' dietary needs are, and how closely tied they are to the population fluctuations of their major prey species.

Interestingly, fluctuations in the Swainson's Hawk population in Schmutz's study area did not correlate at all with ground squirrel numbers, probably because the birds have a more varied diet, depending on other prey items, such as mice, as much as or more than on squirrels.

Ferruginous Hawks are quite efficient at their task of catching ground squirrels. Schmutz estimates that one adult pair of these hawks and their young consume almost five hundred ground squirrels from the time they arrive on the breeding grounds until the time they fly south. This is easy to believe if you've ever visited an active Ferruginous Hawk nest, which almost always contains a decent supply of fresh carcasses.

Ferruginous Hawks have some interesting methods of hunting. They sometimes hover over prey like Rough-legged Hawks. At other times they swoop down on prey from a perch. But perhaps the most unusual method is for the bird to sit catlike next to a squirrel or gopher burrow and wait for a would-be victim to stick its head above ground. On several occasions I've seen migrant Ferruginous Hawks in farming areas of Southern California waiting beside a hole for hours at a time.

Because these hawks spend a great deal of time sitting on the ground, they are sometimes harder to spot than other large hawks. It's advisable to lower your gaze as you drive through an area known to hold Ferruginous Hawks. With their brilliant white breasts, they really pop out if you're looking for them in the right places.

On the prairies of Alberta, which have a good population of Ferruginous Hawks, these birds were traditionally ground nesters. They erected their huge, bulky nests on any available rise, outcropping, or cutbank. After the arrival of European settlers, however, the hawks had to alter their nesting habits. The settlers' herds of cattle made things precarious for the birds' ground nests, which could easily be trampled underfoot. In addition, the number of coyotes—which sometimes prey on the eggs and young of hawks—shot up dramatically with the increase in human settlement.

Fortunately, the settlers planted trees around their farms and homesteads to create shelter from the harsh weather conditions on the prairie. Many of these homesteads were later abandoned during the drought and depression of the 1930s. Today these shelter belts provide excellent aboveground nesting sites for Ferruginous Hawks and a host of other raptor species: Swainson's Hawks, Merlins, Red-tailed Hawks, and Great Horned Owls.

Tree nesting does sometimes create problems for the Ferruginous Hawk. Because the birds are not traditional tree nesters, they lack the innate engineering skills needed to make a really well-constructed nest. The massive structures these birds produce are built mostly from huge sticks or branches, too large to be woven together. They look as though they're thrown together in a haphazard fashion—with the emphasis on *hazard*. It's not unusual for the birds to lose their eggs, young, or even the entire nest in a strong prairie windstorm.

It is always easy to tell the difference between a Swainson's Hawk nest and a Ferruginous Hawk nest, even if the adults are away. The Swainson's Hawk nest is a much daintier affair, woven together with finer branches and often lined with fresh leaves. But nothing is dainty about a Ferruginous Hawk, and the nest is no exception. These birds don't attempt any kind of weaving as they throw the thing together. They do, however, provide a lining, usually consisting of various chunks of sod and cow pies collected from the prairie.

The adult Ferruginous Hawks perform grand aerial displays while courting, rising and diving high in the air, sometimes flipping over and locking feet
together like eagles. It's an impressive show.

The eggs, usually two to four in number, hatch after twenty-eight to
thirty-three days of incubation, and the young fledge in another forty-four to
forty-eight days. As the young hawks grow larger, they often lie in the nest
with their beaks agape, exposing an amazingly massive oral cavity. Some researchers surmise that this behavior and the size of their gapes is part of their
thermoregulatory system, keeping them from overheating in the long, sweltering days of the prairie summer.

With its size, its extraordinarily beautiful plumage, and its fascinating behavior, the Ferruginous Hawk is one of the most impressive of North America's birds. If you ever have the chance to travel across the prairies and open
rangeland of the western states and provinces, be sure to keep an eye out for
this remarkable raptor.

A Peregrine Falcon, the female of the pair nesting on Dundas Mountain, flies above the bizarre landscape of Thule Air Base—a place with the look and feel and all the charm of a NASA outpost on Mars. (Greenland, 1999)

To photograph this young white Gyrfalcon, Bill Burnham and I had to scale a lofty sea cliff without the benefit of ropes, carabiners, ascenders, or other climbing aids. (Greenland, 1999)

A different view of the Gyrfalcon nest cliff. (Greenland, 1999)

Dovekies at a nest colony in northwest Greenland. These tiny alcids, barely the size of a starling, thrive in the frigid waters of the High Arctic, where they dive for zooplankton. (Greenland, 1999)

Arctic foxes often take advantage of Dovekies, prowling around their nest colonies trying to find an adult or chick sitting too close to the mouth of its burrow. (Greenland, 1999)

Looking up at the jagged snowcapped peaks, rising 4,000 feet above the fjord, all I can think of is Valhalla—the sacred place of ancient Norse legend. (Greenland, 2000)

The cryptic colors of a Glaucous Gull chick are a near-perfect match for the rocks behind it. (Greenland, 2000)

An adult Gyrfalcon flies above her nest canyon. (Iceland, 1998)

An adult female Gyrfalcon watches us from a rocky outcropping near her nest. (Iceland, 1998)

These young Gyrfalcons will be the first birds to fledge successfully from this site in three years, thanks to the efforts of Dany Pierret, who came back in the winter and repaired the original nest with sticks and wire. (Iceland, 1998)

Gyrfalcons almost always nest on high cliffs, laying their eggs on grassy ledges or in old raven nests, like this one. (Iceland, 1998)

A freezing wind blows across the mountain as we climb, bringing a shroud of dense fog and the threat of sleet. On the other side of the mountain lies a sheer cliff dropping hundreds of feet below, which Olafur will rappel down to reach a Gyrfalcon nest ledge. (Iceland, 1998)

Rock Ptarmigans are a favorite prey of Gyrfalcons in Iceland. (Iceland, 1998)

A Merlin is one of the most dashing of all North American raptors. Though they're only the size of a Mourning Dove, they catch a wide variety of birds in high-speed chases across open country. (Alberta, 1991)

Prairie Falcons are spectacular flyers and catch a wide variety of prey. In flight, they can be distinguished from peregrines and other North American falcons by their dark axillaries, which form a triangle on their underwings. (Alberta, 1989)

A Prairie Falcon. (Alberta, 1989)

A nestful of young Prairie Falcons, still in white down. (Alberta, 1989)

On a woodland pond in northern Alberta, I got to know this pair of Red-necked Grebes. I spent almost two weeks with the birds during their courting, nest building, and egg laying. (Alberta, 1989)

A nestful of young Ferruginous Hawks. (Alberta, 1989)

An adult American Avocet flies over the estuary at Back Bay Newport. (California, 1988)

One of the world's most beautiful shorebirds, the American Golden-Plover is a common breeder each summer on the tundra near Churchill. These strikingly marked birds spend most of the year in South America, returning to the far north only to rear young. (Churchill, Manitoba, 1997)

In Churchill, the usually drab gray Short-billed Dowitcher assumes the stunning cinnamon colors of their nuptial garb. (Churchill, Manitoba, 1997)

A Willow Ptarmigan at Churchill. (Churchill, Manitoba, 1997)

This juvenile Red-tailed Hawk appears to be standing guard at the boundary of the Upper Newport Bay Ecological Preserve. (Back Bay Newport, 1988)

A young Peregrine Falcon at a nest cliff along the California coast. (California, 1977)

At a pond near Churchill, an adult Pacific Loon performs a dramatic display, arching its back and spreading its wings, splashing water high in the air. (Churchill, Manitoba, 1997)

15

LOST AND FOUND

In November 1998 Pamela Rasmussen of the National Museum of Natural History in Washington, D.C., did something that countless ornithologists and birders have only dreamed about: She and two colleagues rediscovered a species of bird that hadn't been positively sighted for 113 years. Called the Forest Owlet *(Athene blewitti)*, this nine-inch-long raptor is known only from seven specimens collected in India during the nineteenth century. The last confirmed record—a specimen now in the Britain's Natural History Museum—was collected in 1884.

How this rediscovery came about is a fascinating story, involving theft, fraud, and international espionage. In the course of working on a field guide to the birds of the Indian subcontinent, ornithologist Rasmussen became aware of irregularities in the records of Colonel Richard Meinertzhagen, a colorful character who at one time owned what was generally considered the finest private collection of Old World birds in existence. Through painstaking research, Rasmussen and her colleague, Nigel J. Collar of Birdlife

International, were able to show that Meinertzhagen's specimen of a Forest Owlet—which he had supposedly collected in 1914—was a fraud and had in fact been taken from an existing nineteenth-century collection.

So who was Colonel Richard Meinertzhagen, and why is a major scientific controversy swirling around him more than thirty years after his death? He was certainly a soldier: His combat exploits, dating nearly to the turn of the twentieth century, are recorded in detail in his published books and personal diaries. And he was certainly a spy: The official record is murky, but according to his own accounts he assassinated seventeen Bolshevik agents in Spain and attempted to rescue Tsar Nicholas and his family during the early days of the Russian Revolution. And he has been considered the grand old man of British ornithology for years, having written countless articles and several books on birds in the course of his lengthy lifetime.

What happened to bring Meinertzhagen's once seemingly brilliant scientific career into question? An article by Alan Knox that appeared in the journal *Ibis* in 1993 was the first to cast doubt on the veracity of the labels on some of Meinertzhagen's specimens. This raised a red flag for Pamela Rasmussen as she worked on a field guide to the Indian subcontinent, so she and Robert Prys-Jones—leader of the Bird Group at Britain's Natural History Museum—closely checked any of Meinertzhagen's records that seemed questionable.

"I found that Meinertzhagen had fourteen records for the Indian subcontinent alone that were the only known records of those species or subspecies for that region," says Rasmussen. "I had to know whether to include them in our field guide, and that's how I got into this."

Meinertzhagen, who died in 1967, had what he described as a "uniquely perfect" collection of birds—too perfect, as it turns out. According to Rasmussen and Prys-Jones, many of his specimens were taken from other collections at the Natural History Museum. He restuffed some of them, she says, and gave many of them new labels with false data about where they were collected and who collected them.

"In some cases it was extremely misleading," she continues. "There are specimens for which the actual collecting locality is clearly hundreds of miles from where he said he got them. Sometimes the dates are several months off. That can really ruin studies of geographic variation, molt, and more." According to Rasmussen and Prys-Jones, Meinertzhagen's collection has numerous fraudulent specimens, which have probably had a major impact on our knowledge of the birds of India and many other areas where he was even more active.

One of the specimens that Meinertzhagen reportedly tinkered with was a Forest Owlet, which he said he had collected in 1914. This was previously widely considered to be the last specimen record of the species. Rasmussen and Nigel J. Collar say that in fact, the specimen was collected by James Davidson in 1884; it had been taken from Britain's Natural History Museum. "The original stuffing was removed, the bird was washed in solvent to degrease it, and then it was restuffed and relabeled with fraudulent data, as though Meinertzhagen had collected it himself," says Rasmussen. "There are preparation-style features that indicate, without any question, that this was Davidson's specimen. And besides, Meinertzhagen's own diaries show that he never left Bombay during that period in 1914. He couldn't have collected this owlet."

Rasmussen is currently working with Prys-Jones and Collar to sort out the fraudulent bird skins from the authentic ones in Meinertzhagen's Asian collection. Like detectives at a crime scene, they pore over bits of forensic evidence, looking for clues. "As far as we know, nothing similar has been done before," she says. "We have had to come up with new techniques." They have been X-raying specimens and have even started using CAT scans to show that particular specimens were not prepared by Meinertzhagen. She and the others have found a number of bird skins that—like the owlet—had been taken from other collections and restuffed.

Looking at the Meinertzhagen case eventually stimulated Rasmussen and Collar to reevaluate the entire known record of the Forest Owlet. In so doing, they found that of the four known records of the bird in the twentieth century, one—Meinertzhagen's—was fraudulent; two of them, which were supposedly supported by photographs, were actually Spotted Owlets *(Athene brama)*, a common Indian species; and the fourth was an unsupported and doubtful sighting.

As she looked more closely at the few specimens of the Forest Owlet available and at a set of the bird's bones, Rasmussen was shocked to find that the bird differed markedly from the Spotted Owlet, which many people had thought to be similar or perhaps even the same species. "It was so different that we feel it probably deserves to be in a separate genus," she says. "Normally in closely related birds you don't find any osteological differences—usually they're almost indistinguishable. But these bones were so different, I could hardly believe it."

Some ornithologists had considered the bird virtually identical in appearance to the Spotted Owlet and that to identify it in the field you would have to look at its habitat. "However, we studied all seven specimens," says Rasmussen, "and in so doing found that there were quite a few differences between the plumages of these two species that hadn't been made clear in the literature."

Rasmussen also found that the scientific literature on the bird's distribution had been misleading. It was said to be distributed across the Indian subcontinent, when in fact it had been found in only four locations—two on the eastern side of the subcontinent and two on the western side. No records existed for the vast area in between. It also turned out that scientists had previously thought the species occurs only in hill forest, but in fact all of the specimens had actually been collected in lowland forests or valley forests along river systems. A number of searches for the birds had taken place over the years, but the researchers had apparently been looking for the birds in the wrong places. "They were not very close to any of the places where the bird had ever been collected," notes Rasmussen. "So, I thought, there's still hope of finding it."

When Ben King of the American Museum of Natural History—a well-known expert on Asian birds and probably *the* expert on Asian owls—said that he would go to India to look for the bird in November 1997, Rasmussen couldn't pass up the chance to search for the bird with him. Together with Virginia birder David Abbott, they traveled to India and spent ten full days scouring the two eastern sites. No luck. It took two and a half days of driving to cross to the western areas, which seemed less promising because of their relative proximity to Bombay, one of the most populous cities in India. And then they found out that all of the plains forest they wanted to explore had been cleared long ago. They began checking some forested areas in the foothills.

At eight-thirty one morning, as the tropical sun rose into the sky, beating down on the area and raising the temperature considerably, Rasmussen stopped to take a drink from her water bottle. Suddenly Ben King stopped and, almost in a whisper, said, "Look at that owlet."

"I looked up and dropped my water bottle," says Rasmussen. "My voice got high and squeaky, and I said: 'It doesn't have any spots on the crown and mantle!' At that moment we all knew, but we were afraid to believe it. You don't want to be wrong about something like that. Anyway, a few seconds later Ben said: 'It's *blewitti*.' My instant reaction was, this thing is going to fly. I'm not going to be able to verify it, and I'm never going to be able to convince myself or anyone else completely that it was a Forest Owlet."

But Rasmussen and Abbott began videotaping the bird as quickly as they could. As it turned out, the bird was extremely cooperative, staying in place for half an hour before another bird, an Indian Roller, chased it away. They returned in the evening and didn't hear the owlet calling, but the next morning they found another Forest Owlet—probably the first bird's mate—in the same location.

Rasmussen wonders how it could be that this species had been overlooked for more than a century. "A tame, distinctive-looking bird sitting out in the open in the middle of the morning? How could they have gone unseen for so long?" she says. "They must be rare, and they must be local."

Rasmussen is currently trying to arrange a joint research project on the Forest Owlet with the Bombay Natural History Society. "There's a lot to be learned about this bird," she says. "We saw two. That only means that they're not extinct. There are probably populations of them, we just don't know . . . nobody knows. It's really urgent that survey work be done to find out how many there are, where they occur, and what their habitat needs are."

So are there any other mystery Indian birds out there waiting to be found? Yes. The Pink-headed Duck and the Himalayan Mountain Quail have not been seen for decades and, as with the Forest Owlet before its rediscovery, many people believe these species are extinct—but there is no proof.

III

BIRDING AND ORNITHOLOGY

16

WITH THE
SAPSUCKERS IN
NEW JERSEY

May 1992

15 May 1992; 2358 hours; Kearney Marsh, New Jersey. I hear the crackle of broken glass crunching under our tires as I pull off the paved road and park on the dirt next to the railroad tracks. Through the darkness and drizzle, I can barely make out the forbidding shapes of the crumbling inner-city buildings beyond the marsh. I glance at my watch. "Two minutes till midnight. Everyone ready?"

"Sure," says Todd as the other three nod their heads. "Let's do it!"

We all jump from the car and walk quickly across the railroad tracks and down toward the marsh. The ground is thick with tin cans and broken bottles. Shards of glass snap underfoot. We hear something rustling in the reeds as we pass. Ken clicks on his pocket flashlight for an instant, freezing a huge rat in its beam. In our *peripheral vision, the light also illuminates several tough-looking young hoods walking up the tracks. They also freeze.*

"Ten seconds," I whisper. "Five, four, three, two, one. Go!"

At the stroke of midnight we storm to the edge of the marsh and send up a ghastly cacophony of night-bird imitations: ker-wee, ker-wee, kid, kid, kick-kee-do, kick-kee-derr, woc, woc. *The young hoods pause a moment longer, then run off scared into the night. Oblivious to them, we cup our hands to our ears and listen to the marsh.* Quack, *squawks a lone duck somewhere in the reeds.* "Mallard, got it!" *we scream as one and chalk up our first point. The race is on.*

Why, you might ask, are five grown men walking around on broken glass at midnight in a polluted urban marsh in New Jersey, making birdcalls? Because we are the Sapsuckers—the official big-day birding team of Cornell University's Laboratory of Ornithology—and we're competing in the World Series of Birding. Each year in mid-May ace birding teams from throughout North America and Great Britain descend on the Garden State to see which team can find the most bird species in one twenty-four-hour period, from midnight to midnight. The entire state of New Jersey is the playing field, and many teams drive six hundred miles or more as they crisscross the state counting birds in what is perhaps the greatest avian scavenger hunt of all time.

16 May 1992; 0038 hours. A passing nighthawk raises our hopes, making the drizzle more bearable. But the clock is ticking and we're behind schedule.

"Time! Let's go!" I scream and we jump into the car and race to Troy Meadows. Clambering onto a rickety boardwalk, we trudge into the marsh. The boards are slick; some are cracked or missing entirely. Kenny does his famous Sora-with-pneumonia imitation: ker-wee, ker-wee. *Miraculously, a Sora answers back.*

The World Series of Birding and other big-day birding events are proof positive that bird-watching is becoming more competitive. What we now call "birding" is basically bird-watching carried beyond all bounds of reason and common sense. Birders are generally "listers"; they maintain elaborate lists of all the wild bird species they find, arranged according to geography—backyard, region, state, country, continent, planet, et cetera—or by time period: day, year, lifetime. But the "life list" is the most important measure of birding prowess. Some hard-core listers travel thousands of miles to add an unusual tick to their lists—a Siberian songbird that shows up in California; a European shorebird on the New Jersey coast; a South American flycatcher in New York.

I like the British name for listers: *twitchers.* I suppose it refers to the twitch of your pencil when you check off another bird on your life list, but I prefer to picture the Brits twitching spasmodically with excitement and falling to the ground whenever they see a new species. Come to think of it, that description fits a lot of people I know.

16 May 1992; 0141 hours. We drive northwest for miles through torrential rain— windshield wipers flapping at full speed—to reach our "secret" marsh. As we pull over to park, we notice half a dozen other parked cars. Racing down the muddy path to the marsh on foot, we pass several indistinct shapes sloshing past in the opposite direction—the dispirited hulks of other big-day birders. Most pass in silence, except Zeiss/Guerilla Birding Team captain Pete Dunne, who comments, "It doesn't get any better than this."

Mere listing was not enough of a challenge for some birders. So they started doing big days, seeing how many species they could find in twenty-four hours.

Then someone came up with the bright idea of turning this neurotic compulsion into a moneymaker. Like "walkathons," "bikeathons," and various other "athons," there are now "birdathons"—events in which people pledge money for each bird species a team finds on a big day. New Jersey's World Series of Birding was one of the first and most successful events of this kind. The brainchild of famed birder and author Pete Dunne, the World Series is organized each year by the New Jersey Audubon Society. Since 1984 birding teams have turned the Garden State upside down each May, vying for honor, glory, trophies, and pledge money (but mostly to outdo other birders). For one day the teams scour New Jersey, starting wherever they want but always ending up at the Cape May Point lighthouse in an event that makes marathons look tame by comparison.

But why New Jersey? After all, the state is not exactly famous for its wide-open spaces and lack of development. Part of the reason is tradition: As early as the 1920s and '30s famed birders Charles Urner, Ludlow Griscom, and others were trying to see how many birds they could find in the state in one day. At that time there were no teams or competition as such—just one or more bird-watchers trying to set a personal record for the state. Another reason: Pete Dunne lives in the state and works for New Jersey Audubon, which has organized the event from the start. Beyond all those reasons, however, New Jersey has a remarkable diversity of habitats—wetlands, fields, forests, swamps, pine barrens, streams, tidal flats, estuaries—in a relatively small area, and they attract a wide range of bird species. The timing of the event in mid-May takes advantage of the fact that a few wintering birds, such as waterfowl, may still be in the area, most breeding species will already be singing on their territories, and many migratory species on their way farther north will be pausing in New Jersey en route. Consequently, New Jersey is one of the few states where it is possible to find two hundred or more species of birds in a single day.

16 May 1992; 0348 hours. We're still standing in the rain, shivering, with water dripping from our hat brims in a steady flow. The other teams are long gone. But finally, as the first traces of daylight tinge the eastern sky, an American Bittern emits its loud, booming call—oonk-a-lunk—and we happily head for greener pastures to look for grassland birds.

The Cornell Lab of Ornithology has fielded a team every year since the World Series of Birding began. The event has become a major annual fundraiser, bringing in thousands of dollars in pledge money from members and friends of the Lab. This year the Sapsuckers included Todd Culver (Lab education specialist), Kevin McGowan (curator of Cornell's bird collection), Ken Rosenberg (ornithologist and ace birder), Ned Brinkley (a Cornell doctoral candidate in comparative literature and a top Cayuga Basin birder), and me—editor in chief of *Living Bird* and the current team captain. Ken has carried the Sapsucker banner longer than anyone else on the team. This is his seventh time at bat in the World Series and he plans to return next year. (Big days are addictive.) Ken is blessed with a remarkably keen ear for birdsong. During last year's World Series he picked out the high-pitched song of a Blackburnian Warbler—*zip zip zip titi tseeeeee*—as the Sapsucker-mobile raced down the highway at sixty miles per hour. We skidded to a halt and went back to check it out. Of course, Ken had made a good call. Ned is the newest and youngest member of the Sapsuckers. This spring he camped out in New Jersey by himself for a couple of weeks before the rest of the team arrived to start their pre–World Series scouting. He was up by four o'clock each morning to hear the dawn songbird chorus and stayed up well past midnight searching for night birds.

16 May 1992; 0548 hours. We charge up a soggy tractor road to the top of a grassy hill, where the entire valley opens up before us like an immense amphitheater. Here the slightest avian hiccough is audible. "Savannah Sparrow, check!" "Vesper Sparrow, check!" Our list is growing fast. We drop into the valley and stop at an American Kestrel nest near a farmhouse to pick up an easy point. Lesser Yellowlegs, Spotted Sandpiper, and Killdeer around the farm pond are unexpected bonuses. Bobolink falls next, then we blast to Stokes State Forest to find woodland birds.

To rack up a decent score in the World Series of Birding, you must be skilled at birding by ear. Since nearly all bird species have a distinctive song, you don't have to see a bird to count it. If all the team members hear the *chip, chupety, swee-ditchety* song of a Canada Warbler and correctly identify it as such, then it can be counted whether anyone sees it or not. This is particularly useful with night-calling marsh birds, owls, and many forest warblers that call from dense foliage. But great ear birders are born, not made. They have the same perfect auditory memory as a great musician. They can hear a birdsong once and remember it for life. The rest of us have to learn in more mundane ways—listening to birdsong recordings over and over, using picture flash cards coded with recordings, or associating a human phrase with a bird vocalization. (For example, the Barred Owl's call sounds like "Who cooks for you?") But on a big day, you don't have time to go through an elaborate mental process to figure out which bird is singing. You must be able to hear it and name it instantly.

People often ask whether anyone ever cheats during the World Series of Birding. After all, they say, it's all done on the honor system; wouldn't it be easy to throw in a few more birds to win? But cheating is not as easy as it seems. All of the teams get together the morning after the event and compare notes about what they saw and heard. If your World Series list contains some rarities that no one else saw, many people will want to drive out and see them (to get the birds on their life lists). If your list has a lot of species that other teams didn't see, even though they were in the same area at the same time, then your total would be suspect.

But nothing like this has ever happened in the event. And the main reason is that the top-level birders who compete in the World Series have spent years building up their credibility in an activity that is based entirely on the honor system. The kind of people who fabricate bird sightings tend to lose their credibility fast. (How many times can you announce seeing a rare bird that no one else has seen before other birders start ignoring you?) No one like that would be invited to join a team. Besides, this event isn't worth risking disgrace to win. There are no cash prizes; you're in it for the honor, and if you cheat to win, then you lose your honor. And because each team has between four and six members—all of whom have their own personal reputations at stake—it would take quite a conspiracy to produce a fake big-day list and stand by it.

♦ ♦ ♦

16 May 1992; 0900 hours. The weather has silenced many birds and delayed the dawn singing, but we are still heading for a near sweep of nesting New Jersey warblers. Zeee zeee zee-zo-zee—"Black-throated Green Warbler, got it!" Weety-weety-weeteo—"Magnolia Warbler, check!" Zray zray zray zreeeee— "Cerulean Warbler, all right!" A quick jog to some woods where a pair of Sharp-shinned Hawks nests yields the hawks—kik kik kik—a Nashville Warbler— seebit seebit seebit seebit titititi—and a Wild Turkey—gobble gobble gobble.

The most effective strategy for success is to put in a lot of legwork before the actual day—find as many birds as possible that are already singing on their spring territories, then go back on the big day and "harvest" them. The best teams stop no longer than five minutes at each place and have backup areas for as many species as possible, in case an individual bird isn't singing when the teams stop in its territory. If you string together enough staked-out birds, visit enough hot spots, and pick up enough lucky fly-by birds while driving around, you can make a respectable score. But people who don't scout adequately rarely do well in the World Series, even if they're first-rate birders.

16 May 1992; 1030 hours. We sprint to an area where a Ruffed Grouse was drumming during scouting. Ned pounds his chest like Tarzan to mimic the sound. No response. No one thinks it will work, but Ned keeps pounding for a full five minutes. Just as we turn to run to the car, the loud, distinctive drumming of the gamebird rings out through the woods. "Ruffed Grouse, check!"

When you leave the forests and head to the open beaches and marshes along the coast, ear-birding abilities become less important. Here the eyes have it. You must be able to distinguish flight characteristics and field marks of flying birds at the extreme limits of binocular-aided vision. And for shorebirds, it also helps to be methodical and patient as you scan slowly across huge flocks with a high-power spotting scope, trying to separate individual species from the mass. Subtle color differences, bill shapes, feeding techniques, and behavior all offer clues to an astute observer. The same is true for open-country hawks and other coastal birds. It's a visual game.

16 May 1992; 1430 hours. As we pull through the gates of Brigantine National Wildlife Refuge—one of the top birding areas in New Jersey—a dense white fog is rolling in, obscuring birds that we'd seen as recently as yesterday. We spot a rare Peregrine Falcon perched on a tower—the first one the Sapsuckers have ever recorded in a World Series—and a Northern Harrier hunting low over the marshes, but we are missing some easy birds. The Snow Geese we know to be on the far side are invisible in the fog and too far away to hear; the Gadwalls, too, are indistinguishable; and just forget about picking a White-rumped Sandpiper from the flock of peeps.

One of the greatest threats to success in the World Series of Birding is despair—the "Big-Day Blues." You've already worked hard for a week or more during scouting, sleeping only three or four hours a night. And then on the night before the event, you're too excited to sleep at all. By late afternoon you're tired and irritable, your eyes are burning, and you still have hours to go. Anything can throw you into a depression that will threaten the morale of the entire team.

16 May 1992; 1615 hours. The team is close to full-blown despair. Brigantine, which we'd been counting on, has been a near bust. "Might as well hang it up," someone says. "What's the use, anyway?" I try to start a pep talk, but it's hard. "We'll keep on going right up until midnight, chipping away at our species list one by one," I tell them. "We'll find them in the marshes . . . we'll find them on the beach . . . we will never surrender!"

We feel energized as we leave the coast. Our despair is lifting, along with the fog, as we travel inland. At an airport field we see Horned Larks, Eastern Meadowlarks, and one Upland Sandpiper. We drive on. Green-backed Heron falls next, a fly-over. Ditto Little Blue Heron. A short stop at some woods produces a singing Summer Tanager. Then on to Cape May. The fog appears again as we approach the coast. We squint deep into the whiteness and pick out a Yellow-crowned Night-Heron and some more shorebirds. We are still ticking off bird species, despite the weather, despite the fog.

It's strange to think that while you're participating in a World Series of Birding, all over the state at that very moment, in bogs, swamps, forests, beaches, and grasslands, there are people like you, doing anything they can think of—hooting, tweeting, whistling, bellowing, pounding their chests—to get a response from a bird. What do normal human beings think when they run into birding teams? Do they even see them, or are the birders so engrossed in their task that they pass into a weird netherworld invisible to everyone else? It sure feels like that during the last few hours of the World Series of Birding.

16 May 1992; 2240 hours. Darkness falls and still we keep on. Pied-billed Grebe falls next. We cruise past Higbee's Beach to look for night-singing chats—no luck—but we do find Whip-poor-wills and, later, a Chuck-will's-widow. It is now past 2200 hours, but we're all gung ho. At 2311 hours, after making owl calls in vain for fifteen minutes, we finally hear the soft, clear trill of an Eastern Screech-Owl above us. With that, we double over and fall to the ground, laughing hysterically. But Ken suddenly remembers that we are still a long way from the finish line and that late teams are penalized one species for every five minutes past midnight that they are tardy. We stop laughing and race to Cape May Point, filling out the official species list while we drive. As we pull into the parking lot at the lighthouse, the clock reads 2359 hours: one minute to go. I jump from the car while it is still rolling and sprint to the visitors' center. I reach the door, gasping for air. The place is packed with other teams. I hold up my list and try to push through. No one budges. Then someone calls out, "Any more forms to turn in?" "Yes! Yes! Over here!" I scream.

And so another World Series of Birding comes to an end at last. When the scores are tallied up, the Minolta/Watershed Watch Team takes top honors, logging in an astounding 205 species. As always, the winners are New Jersey residents (in birding, the home-court advantage really helps). But there is no shame for the Sapsuckers as we drive into Ithaca the day after the World Series. We set a new team record of 184 species, smashing the old Sapsucker record by 11 species, and we also raised more money than any other team, garnering more than $50,000 in pledges for the Laboratory of Ornithology. And who knows? Maybe next year we can win this thing.

As it turned out, the World Series of Birding I wrote about was my last big-day birding competition. The following year, by chance (I think), my wife was pregnant with my daughter, Clara, and her due date was remarkably close to the competition date. Ditto the next year with my son, Jack. So I retired my captaincy to help raise our children. The Sapsuckers have done fine without me. The current team—Lab director John Fitzpatrick with Kevin McGowan, Ken Rosenberg, Steve Kelling, and Jeff Wells—has soared to new heights. Last year they found a whopping 217 species and garnered more than $140,000 in pledges to help support the Lab of Ornithology's bird conservation efforts. Astoundingly, this did not bag them their long-sought first-place finish. They came in third, only two species behind the overall winner, which shows just how much the bar has been raised since I was a competitor. And they won the Stearns Trophy for highest out-of-state total for the fourth year in a row.

But that's not the end of their saga. On May 12, 2001, the Sapsuckers finally did it. On a tough big day in which only four teams broke the 200 mark, the Sapsuckers amassed a winning score: 214 species. Now the magnificent silver Urner Stone Cup rests on an oak table at the Lab—right beside the Stearns Trophy, which the Sapsuckers get to keep for yet another year. There's only one small shadow on this great victory: the Delaware Valley Ornithological Club's team (which has won the World Series of Birding for the past couple of years) also found 214 species, thereby tying for top honors with the Sapsuckers. So the mighty Sapsuckers still have one more goal to strive for—an unshared first-place World Series of Birding title.

17

A LITTLE NIGHT MUSIC

1996

Each autumn millions of songbirds from across North America embark on an epic journey, traveling thousands of miles, usually at night, to reach their distant wintering grounds in Central and South America. And each spring they repeat the process, returning to spend the brief, warm summer months in the North, nesting and rearing young. The phenomenon of migration is one of the most fascinating and researched aspects of bird study. (Aristotle wrote on the topic more than two thousand years ago.) And yet how effective are our current study techniques? Most of what we know about songbird migration is based on observing or banding birds that have, at least temporarily, dropped out of the migration.

According to Ken Rosenberg, chief scientist of the Bird Population Studies program at the Cornell Laboratory of Ornithology, we may only be seeing the dregs of the migration. "These birds want to go as far as they can, as quickly as possible," says Rosenberg. "They only land when they have to. We really haven't even begun to monitor the successful true migration that goes on every night."

This could all change in the near future, thanks to the innovative work of Bill Evans, who is developing a method of recording and identifying the nocturnal flight calls that migrating birds use to keep track of each other while flying in the dark. According to Evans, these calls—some of which last only one-twentieth of a second—are distinctive and can be used to identify the species of birds passing overhead at night. This could represent a major improvement over existing night monitoring techniques—counting birds that fly across the face of the moon; counting birds that fly through the beam of a ceilometer (a powerful searchlight pointed into the sky); or counting birds with radar—all of which provide data on the numbers of birds flying over on a given night but don't identify their species.

After nine years of independent, self-financed study, Evans published his first paper on night calls in the spring 1994 issue of *The Wilson Bulletin.* In the article he differentiated between the similar nocturnal calls of the Gray-cheeked Thrush and the Bicknell's Thrush by comparing spectrographs of the birds' calls. A spectrograph is a computer-generated "snapshot" of a bird vocalization showing the frequency and duration of the sound. Particular nuances of a sound, often too subtle to be heard, show up plainly in a spectrograph. This technology is the wedge that Evans is using to decipher the brief calls and assign identities to each caller.

Turning a sound into a visible image creates a piece of physical evidence that a computer can compare with other spectrographs to isolate a species' "call signature." The spectrographic image of a species' night call can be as distinctive as a fingerprint, offering an effective way to document the presence of a particular species flying over at night.

In theory, this all sounds remarkably easy: Simply make a spectrograph of every species' nocturnal flight call, and then design a computer program that can recognize the distinctive patterns in each spectrograph and automatically identify the species calling. In reality, Evans's task is much more daunting. The first major stumbling block is correctly identifying all of the nocturnal flight calls. "It's easy to recognize a flock of Canada Geese flying over at night," says Evans. "The geese honk the same at night as they do during the day. But the nighttime calls of songbirds are often very different from their daytime calls. And because the birds are flying in the dark, it can be extremely difficult to determine the identity of the caller."

To solve this problem, Evans has been traveling around the country, recording night calls in areas where particular songbird species are known to migrate through during a given period. So far he's recorded migrating birds in New York, Texas, Florida, and Alabama. Slowly and painstakingly, using a process of elimination, Evans has built up an impressive catalog of nocturnal flight calls, including more than sixty species to date.

Evans owes the inspiration for his acoustic monitoring technique largely to serendipity. A student at the University of Minnesota during the mid-1980s, he spent most evenings working at a pizza parlor to make ends meet. During spring and fall migrations he would camp out for days so that he could watch newly arrived birds passing through the area. "Basically, the whole thing evolved out of my frustration at only being able to go birding on weekends," he explains. "The migration is such a short period. I felt I really needed to be out in the field every day at dawn to get into the rhythm of the migration. And I liked the feeling of waking up at a campsite every morning. I'd sit along this bluff on the St. Croix River and watch flocks of migrating passerines work their way through the trees during the day."

Late one night in May, after delivering pizza all evening, Evans drove to his campsite on the bluff. On this balmy night he lay awake for hours, his mind focused on the sounds of the night, including the calls of migrating birds passing high overhead. Occasionally he picked out a call that seemed familiar: a Black-billed Cuckoo? It sounded like one. And then he heard another. And another. Though Black-billed Cuckoos are not rare, they are secretive and hard to find during the day. And yet he was now hearing dozens of them flying over. Intrigued, he started counting the calls. Within an hour he had tallied more than one hundred cuckoos.

The full potential of the phenomenon he was observing hit Evans with the force of an epiphany. "At that moment I saw the rest of my life unfold before me," he says. "I envisioned recording these nocturnal flight calls and using them to document bird populations for conservation. I literally saw all the key components on that one night. It just overwhelmed me."

Evans knew absolutely nothing about sound recording at the time. He went to an audiovisual store the next morning expecting to be able to buy a tape recorder that would record for an entire night, but he discovered that most reel-to-reel and cassette recorders had a maximum continuous recording time of less than two hours. "The salesman recommended that I buy a hi-fi VCR and record on the soundtrack," he says. "That's been ideal. I can record for nine hours on one videotape."

Evans realized what an important tool his night recording technique could be for bird study and conservation. It could provide a method for monitoring bird populations entirely independent of any other technique and could offer separate corroboration of any declines. What's more, it might be the only way to monitor some of the migrants that nest only in the vast Canadian forests, which have few roads. Evans dedicated himself to perfecting this technique. Working odd jobs to finance his project, he set up seven migration monitoring stations in New York State, buying all of the equipment, finding volunteers to run the recorders, and analyzing every recording himself.

At thirty-six years of age, Evans looks boyish, despite his graying hair. In some ways he is an unlikely figure as a researcher—he has neither a doctorate nor even a master's degree. But what he lacks in "paper" he more than makes up for in his drive and the intensity of his focus. Evans records hundreds of hours of nocturnal birdcalls during the migration—each of his seven stations records for nine hours every night. Between migrations he listens to all of the recordings he has amassed, an incredibly labor-intensive process.

That should change in the near future. Last year Evans became a research associate at the Cornell Laboratory of Ornithology, and he is now working with the Bioacoustics Research Program to develop a computer software program that will automatically identify the species and number of birdcalls on a recording. The Lab has already developed similar "pattern recognition" software for identifying the underwater calls of whales. According to Evans, counting the calls of night-migrating birds could become fully automated. He envisions a time when a researcher could check a computer printout each morning and find a complete listing of the calling birds that flew over the microphone the night before.

What do major ornithologists think of Evans's work? According to Sidney Gauthreaux of Clemson University, who was a pioneer in the use of radar and ceilometers to track migrating birds, the acoustic monitoring technique has tremendous potential. "You'll actually be getting evidence of what's up there," he says. "The calls are probably distinctive enough to be able to identify many of the species that are migrating."

John Richardson, another prominent radar researcher, concurs. "This could be a big advance over what's available now," he says. "One of our major limitations is always that you rarely know what species you're looking at precisely. Nighttime migration studies have suffered as a result. Any technique that would help to identify at least some of the birds going over at night could certainly be valuable by itself or particularly in conjunction with radar. But used by itself, you're depending on the birds to call in order to detect them, and you don't know what proportion are calling."

To make matters worse, some species may not even call at night. "Who's ever heard an *Empidonax* flycatcher calling at night?" says Kenneth Able of the State University of New York at Albany, a recognized authority on bird migration. "What about vireos? Do vireos call at night? Maybe we'll eventually find out that they do, but as far as I know at the moment no one hears them. And yet there are obviously a lot of flycatchers and vireos up there.

"But what this technique does provide, it provides very well," he adds. "It's going to tell us the composition of some of these warbler migrations; it's going to tell us a lot about thrush migrations; it can give us all these things that we don't have any effective way of getting at present."

Evans is actually not the first person to explore the idea of recording nocturnal bird sounds. In the late 1950s and early 1960s Richard Graber and William Cochran of the University of Illinois recorded the night sounds of migrating birds. But their research was ahead of its time, and they eventually ran into a technological brick wall. "We recorded for about three years with old-fashioned equipment," says Cochran. "When we started out, I built a giant reel, bigger around than a basketball hoop. We spliced a lot of reel-to-reel tape together so it could run all night."

Later Cochran, an electrical engineer, designed a timer that would turn the tape recorder on and off so that it would record only ninety seconds of birdcalls every ten minutes throughout the night. "Dick Graber did the analysis, listening to the tapes—all the hard work. The real limitation was not how much we could record but how much Dick could listen to. We finally moved on to other projects.

"Computerizing this technique will bring it into the category of a science rather than just a pastime," Cochran continues. "Automate it and your sample size can become huge, because it's just a matter of replicating some equipment in the field. Bill's got seven stations out now; he could easily have seventy stations soon. The value of the data will increase exponentially with the number of stations.

"Whether or not Bill succeeds with this will depend a lot on how long he can hold up against the forces of entropy," he concludes. "I think his call identifications will be accepted. He's really been looking at this thing with a fine-toothed comb; that impressed me."

Evans is fascinated by the patterns of migration he sees emerging through his data. During the past ten years of recording night calls, most Veeries have flown over his stations in the last week of August, Rose-breasted Grosbeaks in mid-September, and various sparrow species in October. More interesting, Evans has made all of his recordings of migrating Barn Owls (an extremely rare species in New York State) during the first week of September, and he actually recorded two Barn Owls during the same hour at stations more than 125 miles apart. These massive movements, which occur in broad waves, are far from being the random movements of individual birds. Each species appears to have its own migration window that may or may not coincide with those of other species of birds on the same breeding or wintering grounds—a window of about a week when the members of a species reach a state of *zugunruhe* (intense migratory restlessness), ready to set off as soon as the weather and wind conditions are right.

Evans has a broad vision for the future of his acoustic monitoring technique. "I believe that someday we'll have microphone stations stretching all the way from northern Canada to South America," he says. "A researcher will be able to plug into the Internet and follow the migrations of each species on a computer screen. I know it sounds like something from a Jules Verne novel, but I can't see any reason why it couldn't happen."

This coming spring the Cornell Lab of Ornithology's Bioacoustics Research Program (BRP) will set up the first automatic acoustic monitoring stations at two sites on the eastern coast of Florida. Unlike the stations currently run by Bill Evans, which record for entire nights whether birds are calling or not, the on-site computers at the two automated stations will record only actual sounds and eliminate the empty space between birdcalls.

According to BRP assistant director Kurt Fristrup, the computers are capable of performing several functions at once, and they can start working out the call identifications virtually as soon as they're recorded. "The computers may not be able to keep up with the calls being recorded on nights with heavy bird traffic, but we should have a complete list of identifiable calls before noon the next morning," he says.

The two stations will be set up only a mile apart so that some of the same birds will pass over both sites, allowing researchers to measure the flight speeds of individual birds. Bill Evans will also be recording with his original equipment at these sites this spring so that he can compare the data supplied by both systems. If all goes well with the computerized system this year, Evans hopes to have many more fully automated stations in operation by next spring.

"This spring we're just trying to demonstrate the system," says Fristrup. "We want to show that this isn't something that 'might' work; it's working right now, and if we can get sufficient funding we can set up many more stations." Using fully computerized systems will speed up the processing of data to a point that makes it feasible to have dozens if not hundreds of migration monitoring stations in operation. And these systems are designed for online use, so researchers will be able to dial up the computers, collect data, check on their performance, and even reprogram them if necessary right from the Lab.

"This is not a small project," says Fristrup. "We have a lot of work ahead of us. But when you think about what Bill Evans is trying to accomplish—setting up a continent-wide system for automatically monitoring bird migrations—the possible benefits to ornithological research are staggering."

18

SHOREBIRDS IN SPRING

1988

Spring is a time of great change—a transitional period between the cold, dark days of winter and the long balmy days of summer. For birders it is also a time to take a last look at many of the birds that have brightened up the bleaker months and observe the arrival of summer residents.

On the shorelines, estuaries, and mudflats of California, no birds symbolize winter more than the shorebirds that gather by the thousands each year. They seem to represent a time of coldness, whereas the newly arriving songbirds herald the warmth of summer. Still, the shorebirds will be missed. By late March they are already showing their migratory restlessness as they prepare to depart en masse to their far northern nesting areas.

A rising tension is evident as subtle hormonal changes take place. A more irascible nature emerges in many of the birds. Some of them begin to approach each other aggressively—in crouched position, wings down, tails up. They occasionally chase other birds.

Other changes can be seen. An accumulation of molted feathers skimming across the water or blowing loosely across a sandspit is a sure sign that the drab winter plumages will soon be replaced. The shorebirds that have been with us all winter long seem suddenly to blossom into their richly colored breeding plumages. In February they all looked the same, but in late March, as spring officially arrives, a few individuals begin to assume the new colors. The gray-brown feathers that blended so well with the uniform tones of the mudflat are molted, and the birds take on the colors of their far northern breeding grounds—the dark, rich shades of tundra lichens.

In many ways this is the best of all times to go shorebird-watching. Birders have a unique opportunity to see birds in all their plumage phases, from full winter to full breeding and every transitional phase in between. For that reason, attempting to make positive identifications is a great challenge. It is a fascinating time to be out in the field.

The variations among individual birds at this time of year can confound even the experts. It can be frustrating trying to match these birds with anything in a field guide. A good way to avoid at least some of the confusion is to spend a great deal of time watching shorebirds in this transitional season, keeping a keen eye out for the minute changes as they occur.

Though it is virtually impossible to follow the plumage changes of individual birds, you can piece together the transitional stages by observing birds in various phases of the molt.

In late February a few birds can be seen that show the first minuscule signs of advancing spring. Barely noticeable holes or gaps appear on the scapulars where feathers have fallen out, breaking the sleek appearance of the back. Scan the backs closely at this time for the first traces of new feathers as they begin to emerge. Let your gaze travel down to the flanks and up the breasts of the birds. Knots, dowitchers, and a number of other shorebirds get buffy, rusty feathers that begin showing through in bands and blotches.

You can see the progression of the molt in an individual bird as the plumage transition advances from the scapulars, then up its back and from the flanks, up the breast, and finally to the head in front. The plumage has a patchy quality midway through the molt.

As winter gives way to spring, so the winter grays of the shorebirds give way to a variety of hues and patterns to match the summer tundra. The plumage changes not only reinforce interspecies recognition but also serve as camouflage. The dark scrawls and spots on many of the birds help break up the birds' shapes, allowing them to blend in with low-lying vegetation or gravel. Many species nest in open or semi-open areas, such as on gravel bars, and they depend on their body coloration to hide their eggs.

It is a good idea to take frequent trips out to the marshes or shorelines at this time. Many of the places with massive shorebird concentrations are staging areas for the migration. You may not be able to afford to wait two weeks between visits. There is an urgency to the spring migration—a rush to get through. A massive flock of shorebirds can literally be here today and gone tomorrow if the conditions are right. Of course, some individuals may linger into May or even longer, but the massive flocks of winter will be thousands of miles away.

The next time you go shorebird-watching in spring, take a closer look within the flocks. Scan with your binoculars, searching for the odd birds within the group—the ones smudged and speckled with bolder blacks and rusts than the others. If you look long enough, you may be lucky enough to see shorebirds representing the full spectrum of transitional states, from birds with an odd feather on their back or breast to the curiously out-of-place full-summer-plumage birds.

19

SLEUTH

1988

Who says the life of a sleuth is filled with excitement, romance, and high adventure? The truth—at least for someone working in bird law enforcement—is a good deal less glamorous. In his position as senior investigations officer at Britain's Royal Society for the Protection of Birds (RSPB), Peter Robinson spends a large amount of his time peering through a high-powered telescope or binoculars, trying to follow the movements of suspected violators of Britain's bird laws. Such stakeouts often take place in the harsh environments of the Scottish Highlands or the windswept coastal islands. Robinson laments that in these stakeouts the "good guys" must be up long before dawn to get into position for observation, while the "bad guys" can sleep until noon if they like.

When he is not out shivering in the heather, waiting to see someone commit a crime, or interviewing potential witnesses, Robinson can often be found rummaging through musty bird skins and eggs at a museum, trying to match them up with confiscated items to develop a chain of evidence that will lead to a conviction. To do his work, he must be an expert on birds as well as an accomplished sleuth.

Peter Robinson's beat is the entire United Kingdom—England, Northern Ireland, Scotland, and Wales—and his investigations take him throughout the length and breadth of the country, from the metropolitan hub of central London to the remotest offshore islands. Who are the targets of his investigations? Anyone involved in illegally exploiting or harming the birds of Great Britain. Whether they are bird dealers smuggling falcons, finch trappers netting small birds, egg collectors stealing a clutch of rare shorebird eggs, or people willfully shooting or poisoning protected birds, they are fair game for the RSPB.

The RSPB has a unique role in Britain—in bird matters it's almost like a cross between the National Audubon Society and the FBI. It acts as a volunteer conservation organization but also has a law enforcement branch that pursues bird law violators and aids in their prosecution. This has not always been the function of the RSPB. The group was actually pushed by its members into taking an active role in bird law enforcement. The RSPB saw a massive growth in its membership during the 1950s and '60s. As a consequence, more members were witnessing abuses being committed against birds.

"These members were increasingly coming to the RSPB staff and saying that this person has done this or that: What are you going to do about it?" Robinson recalls.

The investigative work of the RSPB has become more and more important in recent years with the increase in bird law violations and the organized commercial exploitation of some species. The RSPB now fills a gap that exists in the British legal system. Unlike the United States, Britain has no national agency like the U.S. Fish and Wildlife Service or even local agencies set up specifically to enforce wildlife protection legislation. It has no government-funded game wardens or other wildlife protection officials whatsoever.

"The uniformed policeman is responsible for the enforcement of all criminal laws in Britain," says Robinson. "That includes all wildlife enforcement."

This can cause obvious problems, because the people enforcing the wildlife laws have had no special training and often do not have any knowledge of the laws pertaining to the birds and animals they are supposed to protect. Their area of expertise is protecting the lives and property of the citizenry and maintaining peace in the community. Many policemen have little understanding or appreciation of conservation values.

"They'll be interested and keen to do something," says Robinson. "Then they'll ask you how much the bird, egg, or skin is worth. When you say it doesn't have a value in terms of money, you can see you've lost them."

The RSPB's role in law enforcement began modestly with the appointment of a technical officer whose job was to pass on reports of specific bird law violations to the appropriate police departments. It has since evolved into a team of six investigators and a full-time coordinator. Robinson has been at the RSPB for fourteen years and has guided the development of the organization's enforcement arm. The RSPB now takes quite an active role in investigations and even prosecutions, sometimes working independently of the police. Acting on tips from informants, the investigators attempt to build a case against a suspected lawbreaker by tying seemingly disparate pieces of information into a solid body of evidence that will stand up in a court of law.

Of the more than fifteen hundred reports of bird law violations the RSPB receives each year, many can be dismissed out of hand. Some are not actually offenses—for example, the group receives many reports of people shooting crows, which is not illegal. Then there are the violations that the RSPB has no hope of prosecuting successfully—someone finds an illegally shot bird, but there are no witnesses. A number of other offenses simply don't warrant a full-scale effort by the group. If they're dealing with a minor offense that will not affect a wild bird population—such as a person keeping a common wild bird as a pet—RSPB investigators will inform the local police, but the group's manpower resources are too limited to take an active role in the prosecution of the case. "I reserve our energies for what I consider to be the important issues—those involving rare birds," says Robinson.

Robinson sees the rise of organized commercial exploitation of birds—pet dealing, taxidermy, large-scale egg collecting for profit—as a serious threat to wild bird populations.

"A dealer is ten times worse than someone who is collecting birds or eggs for his own use," he notes. "Even with birds that are not rare, as soon as you get into commercial dealing, bird populations are going to be affected."

It's amazing to see how far people trafficking birds and eggs will go to conceal their actions. They're every bit as devious as drug smugglers, hiding eggs in difficult-to-search places in their homes or cars. One person was caught with a thermos jug full of eggs wrapped in foam padding.

"One problem is trying to get the police to realize that when they're searching a car for eggs, it's the same as a drug search," says Robinson. "You've got to make sure that all the car windows will roll down, that there's air in the spare tire, and that there's a filter element in the air cleaner."

Egg collecting is a major problem in Great Britain. What makes this activity especially harmful is that the eggs of the rarest species are the most sought-after targets. The RSPB investigators spend a great deal of time trying to catch egg collectors. It is a particularly difficult crime to prosecute because even if eggs are found in a person's possession, the investigators must be able to prove that they were taken since 1981, when the revised Protection of Birds Act was passed by Parliament. Because no method of dating eggs currently exists, the investigators must either witness the collectors taking eggs or find strong documentary evidence. This is why the RSPB must set up elaborate stakeouts or obtain warrants to search through a suspect's premises. During the searches, the investigators are looking for documentary evidence in addition to illegal birds or eggs.

"We're looking for eggs, yes," says Robinson, "but we're also looking for the data—diaries, field notebooks, ordnance maps, ferry tickets. I've been able to establish that people have booked ferry crossings under false names. This is where the detective work comes in. You put all of this together and eventually each of these things adds up to a substantial bit of evidence."

The stakeouts have also been extremely effective. In one memorable case Robinson received an anonymous tip that led him to stake out a known egg dealer's home. He watched the suspect load a bicycle into his car and start driving north. Robinson followed him all the way into Scotland and watched the man and an accomplice board a ferry to the Shetland Islands. The police on the other end were alerted. They photographed the men as they got off the ferry with their bicycles and camping gear but didn't interfere.

Robinson followed them around the island for several days, watching their progress from a distance through a high-powered telescope. They had a very efficient method for finding nests. One man would sit on a high vantage point watching with binoculars as the other man walked below, flushing nesting birds in the coastal marshes. Using a walkie-talkie, the one above would direct the other to the exact location of the nest so that he could take the eggs. Each evening as the men set up their camp, they would put the eggs into a sack and hide it in the heather.

After the men gathered up their eggs and got on the ferry to return to the mainland, the police moved in and arrested them. This led to heavy fines for both men and drew a great deal of publicity.

Such prosecutions serve a dual purpose, punishing the individuals involved and making people more aware of the problems that exist for birds.

"Our purpose is really to identify the major areas of crime and focus public attention on them," says Robinson.

Robinson feels that you can take away some of the incentive for breaking the laws if you can catch a few people and show others the consequences of this illegal behavior: "When you prosecute one person, you are basically sending a message to everyone involved in this activity that this is what you face."

Besides gathering evidence and conducting legal inquiries, the RSPB also engages in private prosecutions when necessary. This is permissible under British and Welsh law, though a court can disallow it under some circumstances. The RSPB investigators will put together the case completely—conduct an inquiry and prepare a report. If it is a simple case with a strong probability of a guilty plea, they will present it to the court themselves. If it is likely to be a disputed case, they will use a team of general solicitors or barristers (lawyers) who have been retained to represent the RSPB.

Private prosecutions are extremely valuable when the RSPB wants to present a test case to clarify the meaning of an ambiguous law. It is sometimes difficult to get the public prosecutor interested in such cases. They are expensive and time consuming to prosecute, and because there is no human victim, it is not always seen to be in the best public interest to pursue them. At such times, if the crime is serious enough, the RSPB will undertake the expense of a private prosecution.

"I try to get into court those cases in which the legislation is unclear," Robinson explains. "If I can get one of these cases into the high court—get them to make a decision about what the law means—then I can take this decision to the 140,000 police officers in Britain and tell them that the law is now clear. That is money well spent."

Although some people have come to regard the RSPB as primarily an enforcement organization, this is far from the full picture. The group is deeply committed to habitat protection and is involved in land acquisition and management. The RSPB maintains more than ninety wildlife reserves. With over half a million members, it is one of the world's largest conservation organizations. It is also involved in education, informing people about the special needs of birds.

The effort to protect Britain's enormous wild bird population is a largely uphill battle—especially considering the small size of the RSPB's investigative staff. But the investigators are producing some tangible results through their work. In one recent case, Peter Robinson arranged a police roadblock and captured some egg collectors as they attempted to flee from Scotland. After a careful search of the suspects' car, the investigators found two recently taken Golden Eagle eggs. These eagles are rare in Britain, so the eggs were rushed back to the nest immediately. One of them hatched, and the bird eventually fledged. If not for the diligence of the investigators, this eagle would never have been anything more than an eggshell hidden away from public view in an illegal egg collection.

20

LOVE AMONG THE REDNECKS

1990

The thing I've always enjoyed most about birding is getting acquainted with an unfamiliar species. I'm not talking about just adding a new bird to my life list. It's never been enough for me to tick a bird off a list, then promptly forget about it and go looking for another new species. If a bird is interesting, I want to get to know the species—to visit it on its home turf; to see how it feeds, reproduces, survives.

This past summer, on a photographic excursion through the province of Alberta, Canada, I made just such a new acquaintance—the Red-necked Grebe. Although I'd seen the species occasionally before on the California coast as a migrant visitor—silent and solitary, in drab winter plumage—I'd never seen it before in all the splendor of its nuptial plumage or heard its unforgettable mating calls.

While exploring the central and northern part of the province, I saw quite a few Red-necked Grebes. They were usually in shallow lakes and ponds, which they prefer as breeding sites. They build floating nests from old, decaying reeds, marsh grasses, and other aquatic vegetation, usually anchored to reeds or bulrushes. The fact that the nest is not constructed on shore provides some protection from land predators.

I had envisioned making an in-depth study of the courtship and nesting of the grebes, but as time went on, my hopes faded quickly. The birds were shy. The nest sites I found were far from ideal for picture taking. Then, just as I was about to give up, I found them—a pair of Red-necked Grebes nesting on a tiny pond beside a clearing that let in plenty of light. They were involved in the earliest stages of nest construction and were still actively courting.

I set up my blind immediately—at first a fair distance away, moving it closer and closer over a two-day period. I finally stopped less than fifteen feet from the birds. Their images filled the frame of my 35mm camera using a 400mm lens. They quickly got used to the noise of my motor drive. Within a day the birds wouldn't even look up when I took pictures. This setup gave me an amazing opportunity to observe the birds closely. And they were great to watch. Sometimes their activities were so fascinating, I forgot to take pictures. Luckily, that didn't happen too often.

The grebes were impressive in their breeding plumage, their necks ablaze with a rich cinnamon red. And they weren't about to let anyone—animal or human—overlook their splendor. The resounding mating calls of the birds echoed almost constantly around the pond, day and night.

These calls have been described variously as *ah-ooo, ah-ooo, ah-ooo, ah-ah-ah,* or *whaaa, whaaa, whaaa, whaaa, chitter-r-r-r-r,* or like the whinny of a horse. I won't attempt to add any of my own impressions of the grebes' love song except to say that it is a loud, raucous, glorious racket. If you bed down too close to a marsh with a courting pair, you won't get much sleep.

The Red-necked Grebes' entire mating ritual is fascinating. Although they don't dance on their toes like Clark's and Western grebes, their performances are equally interesting. One moment the courting birds seem oblivious to each other, quietly foraging or swimming around fifty feet or more apart. Then, suddenly, they appear to catch sight of each other. Letting out a loud squawk, the birds stretch themselves up to full height with crests erect and swim directly toward each other while calling constantly. They move amazingly smoothly and quickly, looking like they have tiny inboard engines stowed somewhere down below.

Just when a high-speed collision seems unavoidable, they each veer to one side or the other and swim off side by side in the same direction. These movements are so smooth and polished they appear choreographed. And the birds never seem to make a mistake in timing or direction change. The whole thing is a noisy and colorful affair, usually culminating in nest-building activities or copulation.

I spent almost two weeks with the birds during their courting, nest building, and egg laying. It was never dull. Up at three-thirty each morning (it gets light early there), I was in my blind—with a camera, tripod, and steaming thermos of coffee—well before the sun cleared the horizon.

Many mornings, though, the sun never quite broke through the mist that often hung over the area. The pictures I took on days like this have a dull, leaden hue that gives me a chill when I look at them (especially remembering how cold it was when I took them).

And then there were those other days, few but memorable, when warm, brilliant sunshine pierced the haze, setting the images in my viewfinder ablaze with color—the birds with their dark eyes glistening and cinnamon necks aglow; the background water a delicate shade of blue; the plants a vivid mix of greens, browns, and yellows. On those days I fired off roll after roll of film, knowing that almost every shot would be a keeper.

The grebes constantly amazed me. One day a hiker passed by too close to the pond. Rather than flying off hurriedly, leaving its eggs at the mercy of gulls and magpies, the grebe carefully pulled some vegetation from the nest, draped it over the eggs to conceal them, then slipped quietly underwater and swam away. I doubt that the hiker even knew that he had passed a nest or flushed a grebe.

The female at this nest laid four eggs, about average for the species. Though they started out bluish white in color, the eggs soon became nest stained. The birds shared the incubation duties.

Unfortunately, I couldn't wait the full twenty-two to twenty-three days for the eggs to hatch. I had other places to go and other birds to photograph in Canada. I sometimes regret that I didn't stay a little longer. I would have liked to see the young birds riding around on their parents' backs. I suppose there's always next summer.

21

THE BIRDS OF
SANTA CATALINA

1987

Soaring effortlessly above the lofty Palisades at the eastern end of Santa Catalina Island, two Bald Eagles come together in an aerial skirmish. The adult—clearly distinguishable with its brilliant white head and tail glistening in the midmorning light—dives threateningly at the immature bird. Just as an impact appears inevitable, the younger eagle flips upside down and shows its massive open feet to the adult. A few moments later the roles are reversed as the immature eagle becomes the attacker. The show goes on for several more minutes, looking more and more like a playful exercise than a dire confrontation.

A quick scan through the spotting scope reveals several other distant eagles aloft in the area—six of them in all, two adults and four immatures. As the morning wears on, they eventually drift off to land on the high crags overlooking the ocean.

The possibility of seeing Bald Eagles is just one of the many things that make Santa Catalina Island a special place for birders—indeed, for anyone who appreciates nature. Though it's less than thirty miles from the skyscrapers, freeways, and congestion of downtown Los Angeles, Santa Catalina is thousands of miles away in terms of peacefulness, atmosphere, and charm. Looking out from one of the island's many azure blue coves, it's easy to imagine that you're on a Greek isle somewhere in the Aegean.

Catalina, as the locals call the island, has a lot to offer. For the birder the island can provide a rare chance to see uncommon species such as Peregrine Falcons, Bald Eagles, Wild Turkeys, as well as numerous songbirds, shorebirds, gulls, and—if you travel there by boat—pelagic birds.

One unusual thing about Catalina is the large number of endemic subspecies it contains—distinctive races of Allen's Hummingbird, Bewick's Wren, California Quail, Great Blue Heron, Horned Lark, House Finch, Loggerhead Shrike, Orange-crowned Warbler, Spotted Towhee, Western Flycatcher, and Western Gull. Catalina is not, however, a place you would visit to add a difficult species to your life list. All the island's resident species also live on the California mainland. What is special about the island is the incredible variety of habitats to be found in such a limited area: chaparral, coastal sage/scrub, oak woodland, riparian. Catalina has plant species that exist nowhere else, including California's rarest tree, the Catalina mahogany.

Some surprising mammals also exist there, such as the island's most famous exotic, the American bison. A motion picture company abandoned a few of the animals in the 1920s after filming a western on the island. Prolific breeders, they are now a common sight.

Although you may not add any birds to your life list on the island, you might spot an island rarity. Just this past winter, the third Merlin ever recorded on Catalina was seen. The White-tailed Kite has also had three confirmed sightings. A Redhead that wintered there in 1985 was the first of its species seen on the island since 1907.

It's fascinating to note which species of birds and animals did (and did not) make it to Catalina from the mainland. Many species are curiously absent. Numerous ground squirrels live there but no rabbits. There are ravens but no crows. Some species that you would expect to see in a particular habitat are nowhere to be found. You can walk through chaparral country identical to that on the mainland without seeing any Brown Towhees. They simply never arrived on the island. It's a classic example of the role of chance in the dispersal of species.

Some characteristics of the island-dwelling species—both behavioral and physical—are readily noticeable. The birds and mammals on Catalina, as on most islands, are less afraid of people. Many species that are shy on the mainland can be approached readily. The foxes on Catalina are particularly unsuspicious. The plants and wildlife there have evolved in virtual isolation. They have faced far less competition from other species than their mainland counterparts. The size and coloration of some of the birds on Catalina also differ markedly from those found elsewhere. Quail on the island, for instance, are larger, darker, and bolder than other California Quail.

The dispersal of bird species to the island is an ongoing process. Some species have only recently become residents of Catalina. The island's first Acorn Woodpecker was recorded in 1955. Since then, the species has become a regular nesting resident. Brown-headed Cowbirds, occasional since 1983, are now well established—for better or worse.

There are a number of ways to see Catalina. It's easy to tailor a trip to the island to fit your time and budget. The most inexpensive way to go birding there is to travel on foot and do all of your birding in the Avalon area. Actually, it's not a bad way to go. The town of Avalon is pleasant and has all of the necessary amenities close at hand—hotels and restaurants, a supermarket, rental bicycles and golf carts, buses, and plenty of birds.

A good way to start is to stroll—or ride a bike—the 1.7 miles up Avalon Canyon to the Wrigley Memorial Botanical Garden. It's a nice place to walk, and you should see a number of birds on the way. The garden itself is well worth seeing. Most of the endemic plants of Catalina are on display there, as well as a fine collection of succulents from around the world. The botanical garden is the best place on the island to get a good look at a diversity of bird species in a short time, especially if you go there in the early morning. The birds there are bold and unsuspicious. Allen's Hummingbirds, Black Phoebes, Northern Flickers, Spotted Towhees, Chipping Sparrows, and occasionally Phainopeplas and Saw-whet Owls can be seen in or near the gardens. In winter Dark-eyed Juncos, Mountain Bluebirds (on the ridgetops), Western Flycatchers, White-crowned Sparrows, Golden-crowned Sparrows, Orange-crowned Warblers, Bewick's Wrens, and others can also be seen.

After visiting the botanical gardens, you can hike up Memorial Road (it begins right behind the Wrigley Memorial) to the ridge for a breathtaking view of Avalon. You'll also have a view of the top of the Palisades, a lofty series of cliffs near the eastern end of Catalina. This is a favorite perching area for Bald Eagles. You can often see them soaring above the cliffs at midday, but a good spotting scope is highly recommended.

If you visit between May and September, you can take a boat ride from Avalon to Seal Rocks near the eastern end. The one-hour trip will provide a good opportunity to see pelicans, cormorants, and gulls. In addition, the boat passes some of the best areas for spotting hunting Bald Eagles. The water off Pebbly Beach averages about two to three degrees warmer than do the surrounding waters. Glaucous-winged, Heermann's, Western, California, and Herring gulls are seen there.

Getting around in the interior of the island is a little more difficult than in the Avalon area. It's possible to hike all over Catalina—provided that you obtain a free permit from the Los Angeles County Department of Parks and Recreation—but the interior is hot and dry, with extremely steep slopes. Only experienced hikers should attempt it. You must have all of your own supplies, especially water, because there is nothing out there for miles. A broad-brimmed hat and sunscreen are highly recommended. Also, be forewarned: The weather is highly changeable on Catalina. It may be hot as a desert one hour and then, in the next hour, a chill fog might roll in. It's best to be prepared for any possibility.

Fortunately, you can get around the interior of the island in other ways. One good way is to set up a base camp at one of the island's campgrounds, then take day hikes from there. Little Harbor Campground sits beside a particularly nice cove. There you can watch coastal birds and hike through the interior habitat.

Catalina Safari Tours, based in Two Harbors at the western end of the island, runs regular buses to all of the main interior campgrounds except Parson's Landing. The company conducts naturalist-led tours for groups of ten or more. You can also arrange extended tours, some lasting a day or more.

The custom tours are flexible. You can make arrangements for your group to be dropped off and picked up at different locations—for example, being dropped off at Two Harbors and picked up in Avalon—to maximize the amount of the island that you can see. Catalina Safari Tours will also help with other aspects of trip planning: setting up accommodations, booking boat transportation, and so on.

Another source of custom birding tours is the Santa Catalina Island Conservancy. Terry Martin, head of the Conservancy's conservation and preservation program, will design custom birding tours for groups ranging in size from twelve to twenty, but a six-month advance notice is required to book the tour. With his extensive background in birds and island ecology, Martin can provide valuable insights into Catalina's unique natural history.

The Santa Catalina Island Conservancy was established in 1972 by the Wrigley family (owners of the island since 1919) to preserve Catalina Island for future generations. It is a nonprofit organization with a mandate to preserve the ecological integrity of the island—its biological communities and also its geological and geographic formations. Since 1975 the organization has owned 86 percent of Catalina, a total of sixty-six square miles of mostly undeveloped land. The Conservancy oversees the island's resources for the controlled use of the general public and also manages Catalina's famed Airport-in-the-Sky.

Santa Catalina Island has gone through many changes since the Europeans arrived more than four hundred years ago. According to estimates, the island was 50 to 70 percent forested at that time, but an army of introduced browsing animals—goats, cattle, bison, and hogs—has had a disastrous effect on the vegetation. Now only 12 to 14 percent of Catalina is classified as oak or chaparral habitat.

Members of the Santa Catalina Island Conservancy hope to reverse the ecological destruction and restore as much as possible the island's native plants and wildlife. Preservation of the island is a trust that employees of the Conservancy do not take lightly.

"Catalina is a real test case," says Martin. "It's like California was in the nineteenth century. You could say it's a microcosm of California. The problems, solutions, and successes we achieve here will foreshadow what you will see in other places.

"Let's face it," he adds, "wild lands in California are not getting any more common. We still have a chance to turn things around here."

The Conservancy is intent on boosting production of some of the endangered plant species on the island. Only seven Catalina mahogany trees existed until the Conservancy grew seventy-four seedlings in a protected grove, safe from the numerous feral hogs, goats, and bison. The group intends to start similar projects with other endangered plants on the island, establishing new fenced groves for particularly threatened species. The Conservancy is also assisting the efforts to reintroduce nesting Peregrine Falcons and Bald Eagles to Catalina.

Terry Martin speaks proudly of the accomplishments of the group. "We are not currently in danger of losing any plant or animal species on the island," he says. "Things are improving gradually. The only way we can go is up."

"Catalina Island is a piece of our history," Martin concludes. "It looks just like California did a hundred years ago. If we work hard, it may be possible to restore it to the way it looked when the Europeans first arrived here."

Finding accommodations on Catalina is usually no problem, with plenty of hotels, inns, and lodges available, though you should make reservations well in advance if you plan to visit in summer. Catalina also has several campgrounds.

To see the island in all of its natural splendor, early spring is the best time to visit. At that time—late March through April—the hills are covered with lush green grasses and wildflowers. The air won't be as parched and dusty as it is in midsummer, and the hordes of vacationers will also be absent. The human population of the island lives mostly in Avalon and swells from a resident group of two thousand people to more than ten thousand in summer with the influx of tourists. The weather is mild in spring, and many migrants are still present.

Although there are several ways to get to Catalina—regularly scheduled airplanes, helicopters, and boats—the daily boat rides operated by Catalina Cruises are the best from a birding standpoint. It's one of the slowest ways to go (about two hours from Long Beach or San Pedro to Avalon), but that just gives you more time to spot pelagic species, such as the shearwaters found there in winter, or to look at the whales, which travelers often spot from the boats. The open-air observation decks provide unparalleled opportunities for viewing birds.

If it fits into your schedule, take the trip to Avalon that goes by way of Isthmus Cove (Two Harbors). It takes about an hour longer than going directly to Avalon but gives you good views of Ship Rock and Bird Rock coming into Isthmus Harbor—good locations for watching pelicans, cormorants, and gulls. The boat then travels along the coast of the island all the way to Avalon, providing an excellent look at the cliffs along the way and a fair chance to spot Bald Eagles and other coastal species.

Santa Catalina Island has something for every budget and time schedule. Whether you just want to spend a pleasant day enjoying the sights and the birds of Avalon or you intend to spend a month backpacking through the rugged interior, you'll be able to do it all on this picturesque island paradise, along with enough after-birding activities to make your stay interesting.

22

EXPLORING ELK ISLAND

1990

Y ou know that Canada is birding country the minute you exchange your U.S. dollars for Canadian currency. Flip over a two-dollar bill and you'll find an excellent portrait of an American Robin on the back. Then there's the five-dollar bill, which has an even better illustration of a Belted Kingfisher. The new one-dollar coins, called "Loonies" by many Canadians, have a beautiful Common Loon sculpted on the tail side.

But the illustrations on the currency are only a tantalizing preview of things to come. Once you get into the field in this wonderful underpopulated country, you'll find a wealth of first-rate birding experiences.

One of my favorite birding locales in Canada is Elk Island National Park. Located in Alberta, the westernmost prairie province, the park is a fascinating remnant of an earlier, wilder North America.

Bison, moose, elk, and deer roam freely in a mixture of habitats consisting of spruce forest, aspen parkland, and wetlands. Beavers are a common sight, building dams and swimming in the lakes and ponds as they have for centuries.

The bird life is no less amazing. A total of 230 bird species have been recorded at the park, including numerous migrant warblers, flycatchers, wading birds, and birds of prey.

Elk Island is not a true island at all. The national park is surrounded not by water but by highly developed farmland, ranches, and housing. In fact, it lies less than twenty-five miles from Edmonton, a major urban center and the capital city of Alberta. This remarkable national park is actually an island in a sea of civilization.

Anyone driving into Elk Island National Park is bound to be amazed by how much the park differs from the nearby countryside. Elk Island is an undeveloped, hilly area encircled by developed flatlands. The park is comprised mostly of "knob-and-kettle" topography—small, rounded hills with depressions nestled among them. The depressions trap water, creating various small wetlands, bogs, and beaver ponds. These areas provide abundant food and habitat for wading birds and waterfowl.

Elk Island's distinctive topography is one major reason that it has survived intact into our century. Simply put, Elk Island was a difficult place to farm, especially considering how much easier farming was on the surrounding flatlands. Though a small portion of the land was homesteaded in the past, the park never faced the kind of massive agricultural development that occurred on the surrounding lands.

The Native Americans called this area Amisk Wuche, or Beaver Hills. It was well named because the area teemed with beavers before white settlers arrived. (And thanks to the efforts of conservationists, today Beaver Hills once again lives up to its name.) The indigenous people traditionally used the Beaver Hills as a wintering area, because the low hills blocked the howling winds and harsh weather of the prairie winter.

The land of Elk Island National Park was first set aside by a handful of local hunters early in the twentieth century. Concerned about the dwindling number of elk in the hills, the hunters fenced off sixteen square miles near Lake Astotin to form an elk preserve. In 1913 the area became a dominion park. Since that time, the area has expanded to seventy-five square miles, all of it fenced.

The fence is one factor that helps to maintain the "island" nature of the park. Large animals are free to roam about in Elk Island, but they cannot go outside the boundaries where they might cause damage to local farms or be hunted.

The forest edges and lakeshores in the park are excellent areas for birding; because they are transition zones, the greatest diversity of species occurs there. In addition to natural wetlands, there are also numerous beaver dams in the park, which create excellent mini wetlands for birds.

As you approach the main entrance gate at the southern end of the park, off Highway 16, you'll find an information center to the right of the road. This is a good place to begin your exploration of Elk Island National Park.

Talk with staff members at the center. They'll advise you where to go to find the particular birds and other wildlife you're most interested in seeing. You'll also find brochures, maps, and useful books. While you're there, pick up a copy of *Finding Birds in Elk Island National Park* by Judith Cornish. Published by the Friends of Elk Island Society, it provides an excellent introduction to the park's bird life. Another useful guide put out by the same group is *Walk on the Wild Side* by Jean Burgess, which has detailed information about the many hiking trails here.

Once inside the park, I usually make a beeline for Lake Astotin in the northern part of the park. It's the largest and deepest body of water within the park boundaries and contains a number of picturesque, spruce-covered islands. At Lake Astotin you can also get set up at the campground if you intend to stay overnight.

The eastern side of the lake has a fine interpretive center, well worth visiting. A spotting scope is set up permanently behind the center so that visitors can watch the waterfowl and beavers that swim past. Birding is great on a nearby boardwalk, where people can walk out over a marsh, observing the variety of aquatic plants up close.

I recently spent some early-summer mornings there, sitting quietly on the boardwalk and getting great close-up looks at a variety of birds. I saw Canada Geese with broods of goslings in tow; several pairs of Red-necked Grebes, enthusiastically courting; two magnificent Common Loons, their distinctive tremolo calls echoing across the still lake; and several species of ducks, all swimming past me at remarkably close range.

At dawn one day I watched two Common Snipe performing their breathtaking courtship flight beside the lake. All around and high above me they flew, first gaining altitude, then diving like tiny feathered missiles. Rushing wind from their power dives vibrated their outer tail feathers, producing their characteristic winnowing sound—a spectacular show.

A number of wading birds can be seen at the park, including Great Blue Herons and Black-crowned Night-Herons, in the surrounding marshes. Actually, the night-heron is a relative newcomer to the park. The species was first sighted at Elk Island in 1958 and is now increasing in numbers. The Double-crested Cormorant is another bird that was rarely observed at the park until recently. Now they are seen fairly often from April through early October at Lake Astotin. Three species of terns—Forster's, Common, and Black—forage for food at the lake, though only the Black Tern nests there. Unlike the Forster's and Common Terns, which live primarily on small fish they catch by diving into the lake, Black Terns are mostly insectivorous, flying over the marsh like nighthawks. They're fascinating to watch. They seem to be on the wing constantly, trying to pick off flying insects over the marshes, meadows, and water.

One of the favorite species for most park visitors in summer is the Red-necked Grebe, the official symbol of the Friends of Elk Island Society. The grebes' loud, raucous courtship calls echo across the lakes of Elk Island each spring as they perform their elaborate courtship rituals. Several Red-necked

Grebes nest on Lake Astotin, within easy binocular range of shore. Their floating nest structures are easy to see as you walk along the shoreline trail. In early summer you might even spot young grebes riding on their parents' backs. In addition to Red-necked Grebes, you can also find Horned, Eared, Pied-billed, and Western grebes. During fall migration the Horned Grebe actually replaces the Red-necked Grebe as the park's most common grebe species.

Elk Island is a gem of a place, with quiet lakes, wooded trails, and spectacular wildlife. It's as enjoyable to visit as many of the truly remote places I've gone to in my life. And yet it's within an hour's drive of the most populous city in the province of Alberta.

23

A BACK BAY
RAMBLE

1989

With its diversity of plant and animal life and its scenic beauty, Upper Newport Bay is always a great place to visit. But the most amazing thing about the bay is its location, smack-dab in the middle of Orange County, California—fast becoming one of the most urbanized, congested areas in the country. In this budding megalopolis, high-rise buildings, luxury condominiums, and massive housing projects are rapidly consuming any open space that the developers can find. After fighting bumper-to-bumper traffic on the San Diego Freeway or driving along the congested stretch of Pacific Coast Highway that runs through Newport Beach, the last thing you expect to stumble upon is a 752-acre ecological reserve.

Called Back Bay by local residents, Upper Newport Bay is a wonderland for nature lovers of all kinds. It is a constantly changing landscape of marsh, mudflat, and open water. A true estuary, the water level in the Upper Bay rises and falls with the tides. The broad expanse of water at high tide becomes a tiny trickle, barely a foot wide, during low tide. The constantly changing conditions create ideal circumstances for a wide variety of life-forms.

On this warm, sunny day in March I turn onto the southern end of Back Bay Drive, go around the first bend, and pull my car off at a small parking area. It is midday, about an hour past high tide. I sit down close to shore with my camera and tripod. A great deal of activity is taking place at the water's edge. Schools of small fish swim quickly around in the shallows, attracting numerous waterbirds.

A dozen or more Snowy Egrets run back and forth near shore, frantically grabbing at the tiny silver-colored fish. The birds are less than twelve feet away but don't pay me the least attention. A Great Egret towers above them, running back and forth like a referee trying to keep up with the action. Rather than hunting for himself, the bird makes repeated attempts to steal from its smaller cousins. Most of the time it is unsuccessful. Several gulls also try to snatch an easy meal from the hardworking Snowy Egrets.

Overhead, several Forster's Terns hover and swoop, occasionally splashing down into the water. They almost invariably come up with tiny fish clenched firmly in their bills. The gulls seem to take particular delight in chasing the terns, trying to make them drop their catches.

The terns are fascinating to watch but tough to photograph. As close as they are to me, they fill up the frame completely when I use my 400mm lens. They are hard to find in the viewfinder, and they rarely hover long enough in one spot for me to focus and fire my camera. Still, attempting to get flight shots of such fast-moving subjects is always an interesting challenge.

Not far beyond these birds, a lone Great Blue Heron stands statuelike among some waterlogged plants. The bird is slow moving and methodical as it stalks its prey, but when it thrusts its head down quick as an arrow into the shallow water, it usually gets a fish.

Above me, strung out along the top of the bluffs that ring the bay, stand numerous houses—a grim reminder of how close we came to losing Back Bay.

As housing prices soared in the 1960s, this remarkable area was slated for massive development. It was to become a huge marina, complete with opulent waterfront homes and condominiums. Fortunately, in the late 1960s the environmental movement was fast becoming a force to be reckoned with by planners and developers.

In California, which had lost almost 90 percent of its wetlands since the first European settlers arrived, the preservation of an area as vital as Upper Newport Bay was definitely worth fighting for. Concerned citizens, led by groups such as the Orange County Foundation for the Preservation of Public Property, the Friends of Newport Bay, the Sea and Sage Chapter of the Audubon Society, and the Sierra Club, lobbied against development of the Upper Bay. Then a controversial land swap between Orange County and a private company, which would have paved the way for development, was blocked by the courts. In 1975, Upper Newport Bay became a state ecological reserve managed by the California Department of Fish and Game.

More recently there has been more good news for conservationists who seek to preserve this vital area. In late July 1989 the Irvine Company—the present owner of the land—is slated to turn over an additional 117 acres along the northern boundaries of the bay. This area will become the Upper Newport Bay Regional Park. Plans for the park include a nature center and several strategic overlooks for wildlife viewing.

As the water gradually recedes from the edges of the bay, exposing more and more brightly glistening mud, the wading birds move toward the center of the channel. A lone avocet wades past, head down, sweeping its bill from side to side in the mud as it probes for food. I notice that the bird is showing the first cinnamon blush of its breeding plumage—a nice change from the stark black-and-white coloration of winter. The avocet pauses for an instant and stands erect as it hears the whir of my camera's motordrive. Seeing all is well, it continues on its way.

I finally pick up my equipment and move to another part of the bay. Although it is possible to drive or cycle all the way up Back Bay Drive, I decide to walk. It's a beautiful spring day, and the air is filled with birdsong. During my walk, I see Song Sparrows, White-crowned Sparrows, Marsh Wrens, Anna's Hummingbirds, and Belding's Savannah Sparrows. At the edge of the channel I see two kinds of teal—Green-winged and Cinnamon—poking around in the mud. There are also American Avocets and Black-necked Stilts.

I stop near the end of San Joaquin Hills Road to see if I can see any interesting waterfowl there. A few tame Mallards walk toward me, hoping for a handout. I ignore them, and they soon give up and go back to sleep in the warm sunlight. Beyond them are wild ducks: American Wigeon, Green-winged Teal, Northern Shoveler, and a lone drake Blue-winged Teal, looking striking with the distinctive white crescents on the sides of his head.

My next stop along the road is the small boat-launching area—a great place to watch shorebirds from fall through spring. Sandpipers, stilts, dowitchers, godwits, curlews, avocets, and more can be seen here at fairly close range. It is excellent for shorebird photography.

Today two busloads of schoolchildren are visiting the area. A couple of naturalists patiently explain the concepts of ecology while showing the children sandpipers through the spotting scope. Upper Newport Bay is a valuable educational resource for schools in the region. Students throughout the county and beyond get an effective introduction to biology as they study the diverse habitats of Back Bay.

Six distinct habitat types exist at Back Bay: marine, intertidal, brackish water, freshwater marsh, riparian, and upland. All play host to a remarkable selection of bird life. The best times for birding run from late August through early April, when migrants and winter residents are usually present in good numbers.

As early as mid-August, southbound migrants start showing up at Back Bay, particularly shorebirds. At this time, Black-bellied Plovers still in breeding plumage can be seen. Dowitchers, knots, sandpipers—all retain some of the red-brown plumage tones they sported on their breeding grounds.

Waterfowl begin dominating the estuary in early fall. The mild southern California winter brings many overwintering species, such as Elegant Terns and Virginia Rails. Lincoln's Sparrows are frequent winter visitors. Several species of grebes are winter residents: Western, Clark's, Horned, Eared, and Pied-billed. In January 1989 a Bald Eagle paid a one-day visit to the bay, the second record in the decade for this area.

A report on Upper Newport Bay wouldn't be complete without mentioning the bay's premier species, the Clapper Rail. The existence of the bay's resident clappers was one of the most convincing arguments for making the bay into an ecological reserve. An environmental impact study determined that Back Bay holds the world's largest nesting population of the lightfooted subspecies of Clapper Rail (*Rallus longirostris levipes*). And without question, this is the best site available anywhere for viewing this secretive species, especially during exceptionally high tides.

Other marsh species readily seen around the reed beds are the Sora, Marsh Wren, and the endangered Belding's race of Savannah Sparrow. Almost every spring brings a hopeful report of a Black Rail. Although this species could well inhabit Back Bay, no confirmed observations have been made there since the 1960s. Most experienced Back Bay birders believe that the perennial "Black Rail" sightings are probably Coot or Clapper Rail chicks.

In the arid scrub bordering the wetlands of Upper Newport Bay live numerous chaparral-dwelling birds. Life listers will be interested in the California Gnatcatcher. This bird of the coastal scrub was formerly considered a subspecies of the Black-tailed Gnatcatcher, but it recently gained full species status. Listen for this bird's kitten-mew-like call in the upland brush behind the freshwater impoundment about halfway along Back Bay Drive.

Two newcomer species have been added to the attractions at Back Bay in recent years—Black Skimmers and Least Terns—both of which now nest there. Their arrival is probably the result of shrinking wetlands throughout the heavily populated and overdeveloped Southland.

I walk across the road to the freshwater pond and marsh on the eastern side. Scanning the water with my binoculars, I see Mallards, American Wigeons, Ruddy Ducks, American Coots, Common Moorhens, and also a few Canvasbacks in the back near the reeds. I scope in on a drake Canvasback, his crimson eye aglow in the warm spring sunlight. This pond usually has a fair number of Northern Pintails, some of which will let you get amazingly close. I see no pintails here today, though. Perhaps most of them have already left for their northern breeding grounds.

Among the reeds I see a Common Yellowthroat, but it quickly hops down out of my sight. A few Red-winged Blackbirds call noisily, advertising their presence to prospective mates. I see some males gliding along with their gaudy red epaulets puffed out for all to see. Two of them get into a minor territorial scrap, locking feet and tumbling momentarily into the green reeds before separating.

I walk around the entire pond and through the riparian habitat on the northeastern side. I see Killdeers, Anna's Hummingbirds, House Finches, another Common Yellowthroat, and a Red-shouldered Hawk.

Leaving the willows, I continue on my way up Back Bay Drive. As I stroll beneath the dirt bluffs that rise up along the right of the drive, I spot a Turkey Vulture gliding quickly toward me at ridgetop level. These birds are often seen here, along with Red-tailed Hawks, as they try to catch updrafts from the cliff face. Less than a month earlier I saw an adult Peregrine Falcon flying along the same stretch of cliff. The falcon was so close as it flew over me, I could see that a couple of primaries on one of its wings had broken tips.

I stop again near the top of the bay. On a sign marking the boundary of the reserve sits an immature Red-tailed Hawk. It is unusually approachable. I move to within thirty feet, snapping several photographs before it flies off.

Looking out over the bay, I scan the broad expanse with my 10x binoculars. By now, low tide is quickly approaching. The area has become a vast expanse of wet mud, glistening brightly in the sunlight. In the distance I spot a Northern Harrier working the far side of the estuary in its characteristic flight, swooping along low, stalling, half hovering at times, searching for an unsuspecting rodent or bird to pounce on.

The channel that was so wide and full when I arrived a few short hours ago is now only a trickle. I hike back down the road to my car, listening to bird-songs and calls as I go.

As always, it has been a rewarding, tension-relieving experience to walk quietly along Back Bay Drive, sharing this protected sanctuary with its inhabitants. In the urban chaos of Southern California, Upper Newport Bay is a welcome oasis of tranquility.

24
CAN THE EVERGLADES ENDURE?

1993

I'm always astounded when I visit the Everglades. Even while flying above it en route to Miami, the place is impressive, stretching nearly as far as the eye can see in every direction. But at ground level the Everglades is a birder's dream: a place of unparalleled natural beauty, full of wildlife—Wood Storks, Roseate Spoonbills, countless herons and egrets, alligators, and more. Hard to imagine that this great wetland is in danger or that the huge flocks of wading birds that now inhabit the Everglades represent but a fraction of the numbers that once darkened the skies here.

A century ago the Everglades was an immense wilderness of saw grass blanketed by a thin, slow-moving sheet of water almost fifty miles wide. This vast "river of grass" lay virtually undisturbed. But even in the late nineteenth century developers were making plans to reclaim the Everglades—to turn this "worthless" swamp into productive farmland. In the decades since, large portions of the original Everglades have been cut by canals and ditches, blocked by levees, and drained till they're as high and dry as a Kansas prairie. And now the entire Everglades watershed—including the 1.4 million acres designated as a national park in 1947—is threatened with ecological ruin.

But what are the causes of this impending disaster? And what can be done to rescue this irreplaceable national treasure? One thing is certain: All of the problems facing the Everglades can be reduced to a single factor—water. If the quality, supply, distribution, and timing of the water can be returned to something even remotely resembling the original flow, then there is yet hope for the remaining Everglades.

Restoring the natural water conditions will not be easy. The entire northern section of the Everglades has been unalterably changed, and this affects the whole Everglades watershed. Originally Lake Okeechobee spilled over its southern banks and flowed in a broad, shallow swath all the way to Florida Bay, 100 miles to the south. But the U.S. Army Corps of Engineers built a dike along the southern edge of the lake, then constructed an elaborate system of levees, canals, and impoundments to control the flow of water. A 700,000-acre portion of the northern Everglades below Lake Okeechobee was drained to form the Everglades Agricultural Area (EAA), where most of Florida's sugarcane is now grown.

The EAA is the center of a bitter controversy over water quality in the Everglades. Nutrient-rich runoff from cropland is entering the Everglades ecosystem, causing radical changes in the plant community. Agricultural practices are to blame. Farmers pump the surface water from their fields underground and maintain the water level two feet below soil level. Plowing then exposes the peat soil to oxygen, which allows microbes to feed on it. The microbial process releases nitrogen and phosphorus in forms that the plants can readily use as nutrients. Because the soil is porous, rainwater hits the surface and percolates down, moving though the soil and picking up the nutrients released by the microbial action. By the time the runoff reaches drainage canals on the way to the southern Everglades it is inundated with nitrogen and phosphorus.

Although high concentrations of these nutrients would not harm some ecosystems, the Everglades is an oligotrophic system—deficient in plant nutrients. The Everglades plant community evolved for the most part living only on the nitrogen and phosphorus found in rainwater. According to Paul Parks, director of Foreverglades, a program of the Florida Wildlife Federation, the natural background phosphorus in the area was approximately seven to ten parts per billion, whereas the runoff water now averages two hundred parts per billion.

"The natural Everglades has a lot of biomass, but it doesn't grow very fast," says Parks. "When you pump this high-phosphorus, high-nitrogen water into that kind of system, the plant community changes radically."

Cattails are the main beneficiary of the nutrient-rich runoff. They are spreading rapidly, choking out the natural saw grass community. The only places cattails formerly occurred in the Everglades were in small alligator holes, where bird and animal droppings had released nutrients, or in areas where fire had burned the peat soil. In Loxahatchee National Wildlife Refuge more than 6,000 acres are clogged with cattails. Paul Parks estimates that between 30,000 and 50,000 acres have been affected by the farm runoff to date. He warns that if nothing is done, the entire Everglades system could eventually go under.

"When you dump this much phosphorus and the cattails ultimately dominate, every one of the Everglades habitats except tree islands is affected," says Parks. "Saw grass is replaced; wet prairie is replaced. The cattails will even grow on floating mats in the deep water of sloughs."

In the warm, year-round sunshine of Florida the cattails are remarkably prolific. They grow up to twelve feet tall, packed together tightly. Such an enormous pile of organic material falls into the water that the re-aeration process can't keep up with it. An organic goo forms in which small fish can't survive.

"What you have where the cattails grow is just biological trash," says Parks. "There's nothing for birds to eat in it. And they wouldn't waste their energy wading through those dense cattails even if there were something to eat. The open areas the wading birds depend on are getting covered up by cattails."

But fighting for the water quality of the Everglades has meant taking on the powerful sugar industry. One of the cruelest ironies is that sugar farming in the Everglades area would probably not be economically feasible if not for government price supports and restrictive tariffs levied against Caribbean sugar producers. Even in this age of free trade, the sugar industry has been powerful enough politically to keep trade restrictions affecting sugar imports largely intact. The American consumer, who must pay up to three times the world average for sugar products, is one of the primary losers in the affair. Other losers are the tiny Caribbean nations whose economies depend on sugar exports.

Until October 1988 the sugar industry had fought environmentalists to a standstill on the Everglades water-quality issue, managing to maintain the status quo despite overwhelming scientific evidence of the harm being caused by their farming practices. Then a remarkable event took place. The U.S. Attorney for Florida, Dexter W. Lehtinen, filed a federal lawsuit against the Florida Department of Environmental Regulation and the South Florida Water Management District, accusing the two agencies of breaking state and federal law by allowing polluted agricultural runoff to flow into Everglades National Park.

The state agencies dragged their feet for more than two years, in the process wasting six million dollars of taxpayer money in litigation. Then another fortuitous event occurred: Lawton Chiles was elected governor. He and his staff are showing much more willingness to work with environmentalists to solve the water quality issue than the previous administration.

In February 1991 the Federal District Court agreed to delay the lawsuit, pending an out-of-court agreement being reached by both parties. In exchange for the delay, Florida pledged to help federal scientists prepare an Everglades cleanup plan. South Florida water managers have already approved a plan that would flood 72,000 acres of farmland at the southern end of the EAA. The idea is to create a flow-through marsh that will filter phosphorus from the water before it reaches the Everglades. The sugar industry has agreed to contribute four million dollars a year for a decade to the cleanup program.

The Everglades Environmental Protection District will assess farmers ten dollars per acre each year, eight dollars of which will go toward the cost of the cleanup. But the cleanup process may end up costing as much as five hundred million dollars. One sticking point in working out the agreement is that some people feel the sugar industry is making too small a contribution to the cleanup effort. But most people involved in the case feel positive about the eventual outcome.

"It's all looking like it can be done," says Parks. "The tide has turned. We were getting stonewalled for a long time. The thing that broke the deadlock was the federal lawsuit."

If the water cleanup is effective, a great deal of potential damage to the Everglades National Park should be averted. However, the most immediate problem facing the park—which encompasses approximately 64 percent of the original Everglades—is not so much one of water quality at this point as it is of water supply and distribution. According to park biologist John Ogden, program manager for wildlife research, few vegetation changes have taken place yet in the southern Everglades.

"What has really had a massive impact on the wildlife in the park during the last forty years has been the changes in water volume and also changes in the timing and distribution of the water," says Ogden.

In the 1950s and '60s when most of the levee system in the central Everglades had been completed, explains Ogden, the area went through a devastating dry period. To make matters worse, an adequate water delivery system for the park had not yet been worked out. The southern Everglades experienced five or six years of serious overdrainage.

The U.S. Army Corps of Engineers attempted to solve the problem by building a levee and a canal along the eastern boundary of the park. The idea was to force all the water into the park rather than allowing it to spread out over the full Everglades area. What that did was take the same amount of water that had previously flowed across in a fifty-mile-wide band and compress it into a much smaller area, also shifting the water considerably west from where it normally flowed.

According to Ogden, the water project had a devastating effect on wildlife, especially the large flocks of wading birds for which the Everglades was famous. The total numbers of nesting wading birds in the Everglades declined from an average of about 100,000 birds a year in the 1930s and '40s to about 5,000 a year now. Wood Storks, a closely monitored species at the park, declined from between 8,000 and 10,000 nesting birds a year to about 500 during the same period.

"The project changed the water distribution and drying patterns throughout the southern Everglades basin," Ogden says. "Traditional wading bird rookeries were no longer next to water. Places that used to have deep water were now dry. Other places that used to be dry were covered with water. It completely changed the timing of drying."

Ogden believes that if the natural distribution patterns, flow patterns, and timing of the water can be reestablished, a lot of wildlife populations at the park should recover. Some major obstacles to restoring a natural water flow to the park have recently been overcome. Congress has authorized the purchase of 107,600 acres of land along the eastern side of the national park. The U.S. Army Corps of Engineers plans to remove the canal and levee from the park boundary, thus allowing a natural sheet flow of water into the area. The project will restore more than 75,000 acres of wetland, which includes 25 percent of the Wood Stork's original feeding grounds.

Though it will take several years for the Corps to complete the project, Ogden is hopeful about the future of the Everglades. "I've been around here long enough to have seen it when it had a lot more wildlife than it does now," he says. "I know the excitement of the place when it had the big rookeries. We have a real potential for bringing it back—at least to the way it was in the 1950s. There seems to be a real commitment now, and an understanding of what needs to be done. We didn't have either ten years ago."

Can the Everglades be saved? It may be too early to say, but conditions have never been better politically than they are now. President Clinton has pledged that his administration will be attentive to conservation issues. The newly appointed heads of the Environmental Protection Agency and the Justice Department both come from Florida and are familiar with the ecological problems of the Everglades. But perhaps the most promising sign came this past February in a speech delivered by Secretary of the Interior Bruce Babbitt at the Everglades Coalition Conference in Tallahassee. Babbitt offered his full support for the preservation of the Everglades and said that he would form a federal Everglades Task Force to shepherd the controversial cleanup plan to completion. "The Everglades is a test case for all of the ecosystems in the entire country," said Babbitt. "This is the one that needs attention now."

In light of recent developments, reading this essay again was enough to give me twinges of sadness and regret. Instead of Lawton Chiles, we have Jeb Bush as governor of Florida. Instead of Bill Clinton or Al Gore, we have George W. Bush as president of the United States—after an election, ironically, determined by Florida.

At first glance it looks like an unqualified defeat for environmentalists. But is it? Conservation organizations are reporting a new surge in membership and contributions as more and more people realize that the new president will be less protective of our nation's natural treasures than the previous administration. What I find extremely encouraging is that a large portion of the public is strongly opposed to oil exploration in the Arctic National Wildlife Refuge and other environmental outrages. Perhaps this renewal of enthusiasm and activism will be enough to keep America headed in an environmentally sound direction.

As for the Everglades, the situation is still hopeful. In the final months of 2000, both the U.S. Senate and the House of Representatives approved a $7.8 billion plan to restore the Everglades. And as one of his final acts in office, President Clinton signed the bill on December 12, 2000, giving final approval to one of the largest environmental restoration projects in the nation's history.

Of course, I don't think the well-being of the Everglades is something that we will ever be able to take for granted and mark CASE CLOSED, PROBLEM SOLVED. As with the Arctic National Wildlife Refuge, we will have to watch events closely as they unfold and be forever ready to fight to preserve these irreplaceable areas. Otherwise the only "parts unknown" our children will ever see will be epitaphs written in books about places that no longer exist.

INDEX